AMERICA'S PRISONS

OPPOSING VIEWPOINTS®

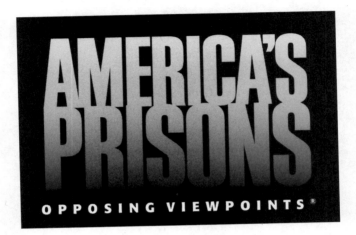

Other Books of Related Interest

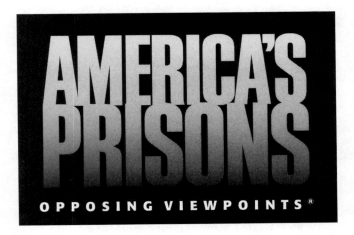

AMERICA'S PRISONS

OPPOSING VIEWPOINTS®

Roman Espejo, *Book Editor*

Daniel Leone, *Publisher*
Bonnie Szumski, *Editorial Director*
Scott Barbour, *Managing Editor*

OPPOSING
VIEWPOINTS®
SERIES

Greenhaven Press, Inc., San Diego, California

Cover photo: California Department of Corrections

Library of Congress Cataloging-in-Publication Data

America's prisons / Roman Espejo, book editor.
   p. cm. — (Opposing viewpoints series)
   Includes bibliographical references and index.
   ISBN 0-7377-0787-9 (pbk. : alk. paper) —
ISBN 0-7377-0788-7 (lib. : alk. paper)
   1. Prisons—United States. 2. Imprisonment—United States.
3. Alternatives to imprisonment—United States. 4. Criminals—
Rehabilitation—United States. I. Espejo, Roman, 1977–
II. Series. III. Opposing viewpoints series (Unnumbered)

HV9471 .A488 2002
365'.973—dc21
                                                    2001023814
                                                         CIP

Greenhaven Press, Inc., P.O. Box 289009
San Diego, CA 92198-9009

"Congress shall make
no law...abridging the
freedom of speech, or of
the press."

First Amendment to the U.S. Constitution

The basic foundation of our democracy is the First
Amendment guarantee of freedom of expression.
The Opposing Viewpoints Series is dedicated to the
concept of this basic freedom and the idea that it is
more important to practice it than to enshrine it.

Contents

Why Consider Opposing Viewpoints?

"The only way in which a human being can make some approach to knowing the whole of a subject is by hearing what can be said about it by persons of every variety of opinion and studying all modes in which it can be looked at by every character of mind. No wise man ever acquired his wisdom in any mode but this."

John Stuart Mill

In our media-intensive culture it is not difficult to find differing opinions. Thousands of newspapers and magazines and dozens of radio and television talk shows resound with differing points of view. The difficulty lies in deciding which opinion to agree with and which "experts" seem the most credible. The more inundated we become with differing opinions and claims, the more essential it is to hone critical reading and thinking skills to evaluate these ideas. Opposing Viewpoints books address this problem directly by presenting stimulating debates that can be used to enhance and teach these skills. The varied opinions contained in each book examine many different aspects of a single issue. While examining these conveniently edited opposing views, readers can develop critical thinking skills such as the ability to compare and contrast authors' credibility, facts, argumentation styles, use of persuasive techniques, and other stylistic tools. In short, the Opposing Viewpoints Series is an ideal way to attain the higher-level thinking and reading skills so essential in a culture of diverse and contradictory opinions.

In addition to providing a tool for critical thinking, Opposing Viewpoints books challenge readers to question their own strongly held opinions and assumptions. Most people form their opinions on the basis of upbringing, peer pressure, and personal, cultural, or professional bias. By reading carefully balanced opposing views, readers must directly confront new ideas as well as the opinions of those with whom they disagree. This is not to simplistically argue that everyone who reads opposing views will—or should—change his or her opinion. Instead, the series enhances readers' understanding of their own views by encouraging confrontation with opposing ideas. Careful examination of others' views can lead to the readers' understanding of the logical inconsistencies in their own opinions, perspective on why they hold an opinion, and the consideration of the possibility that their opinion requires further evaluation.

Evaluating Other Opinions

To ensure that this type of examination occurs, Opposing Viewpoints books present all types of opinions. Prominent spokespeople on different sides of each issue as well as well-known professionals from many disciplines challenge the reader. An additional goal of the series is to provide a forum for other, less known, or even unpopular viewpoints. The opinion of an ordinary person who has had to make the decision to cut off life support from a terminally ill relative, for example, may be just as valuable and provide just as much insight as a medical ethicist's professional opinion. The editors have two additional purposes in including these less known views. One, the editors encourage readers to respect others' opinions—even when not enhanced by professional credibility. It is only by reading or listening to and objectively evaluating others' ideas that one can determine whether they are worthy of consideration. Two, the inclusion of such viewpoints encourages the important critical thinking skill of objectively evaluating an author's credentials and bias. This evaluation will illuminate an author's reasons for taking a particular stance on an issue and will aid in readers' evaluation of the author's ideas.

It is our hope that these books will give readers a deeper understanding of the issues debated and an appreciation of the complexity of even seemingly simple issues when good and honest people disagree. This awareness is particularly important in a democratic society such as ours in which people enter into public debate to determine the common good. Those with whom one disagrees should not be regarded as enemies but rather as people whose views deserve careful examination and may shed light on one's own.

Thomas Jefferson once said that "difference of opinion leads to inquiry, and inquiry to truth." Jefferson, a broadly educated man, argued that "if a nation expects to be ignorant and free . . . it expects what never was and never will be." As individuals and as a nation, it is imperative that we consider the opinions of others and examine them with skill and discernment. The Opposing Viewpoints Series is intended to help readers achieve this goal.

David L. Bender and Bruno Leone,
Founders

Greenhaven Press anthologies primarily consist of previously published material taken from a variety of sources, including periodicals, books, scholarly journals, newspapers, government documents, and position papers from private and public organizations. These original sources are often edited for length and to ensure their accessibility for a young adult audience. The anthology editors also change the original titles of these works in order to clearly present the main thesis of each viewpoint and to explicitly indicate the opinion presented in the viewpoint. These alterations are made in consideration of both the reading and comprehension levels of a young adult audience. Every effort is made to ensure that Greenhaven Press accurately reflects the original intent of the authors included in this anthology.

Introduction

"Drug abuse is a health, moral, and spiritual problem; it is time to stop treating it as a criminal problem."
—Doug Bandow, Christian Science Monitor,
December 11, 2000

"For many addicted individuals, it is important to have enforcement—incarceration—attached to treatment."
—Dick Spees, *quoted in the* San Francisco Recorder,
November 3, 2000

The United States is often described as a punitive nation. Population growth alone cannot explain the phenomenal growth of its prison system. While the nation contains only 5 percent of the global population, its prisons now house 25 percent of the world's inmates. On February 15, 2000, the U.S. prison population reached 2 million, according to the Justice Policy Institute, doubling in only a decade. Currently, sixteen states have lower populations than the number of people incarcerated in the nation's correctional facilities.

Many crime experts favor these high rates of incarceration, arguing that America is the most violent of industrialized nations. For instance, the U.S. Department of Justice reports that the chance of being murdered in the United States is about six times higher than in England. Supporters insist that incarcerating more offenders for longer periods of time is the best way to maintain public safety. A study conducted by economist Steve Levitt found that an additional fifteen crimes each year occur every time an inmate is released from prison due to overcrowding.

However, critics of the prison system maintain that America's crime rate does not exceed those of similar nations; therefore its high imprisonment rates are not justified. For example, a survey conducted by the Dutch Ministry of Justice found that Australia, Canada, the Netherlands, and New Zealand had higher incidences of eleven types of crime than the United States, including robbery, burglary, and car theft. Critics attribute America's prison population boom not to an epidemic of crime, but to harsher sentencing laws and the nation's war on drugs, characterized by increased antidrug efforts and stiffer penalties for drug offenders. Marc Mauer, assistant director of the Sentencing Project, maintains that "in 1980, 6 percent of inmates were in for drug offenses. That's up to 21 percent in 2000."

Because of chronic prison overcrowding and the rapid expansion of the prison system, the nation's penal policies have been intensely scrutinized, especially those dealing with drug offenders. Near the end of his second term, former President Bill Clinton said, "We really need a re-examination of our entire policy on imprisonment. . . . There are tons of people in prison who are nonviolent offenders—who have drug related charges that are directly related to their own drug problems." Many critics of the prison system contend that 1 million of these offenders languish behind bars, trapped by rigid mandatory sentences aimed at incapacitating the worst offenders. They also add that drug abuse runs rampant in prison, and most incarcerated drug addicts receive little or no treatment.

Various states are experimenting with alternative sanctions for drug offenders. In recent years, the number of drug courts, where judges stringently monitor drug offenders' probation, have spread across the country. In 1996, Arizona voters approved Proposition 200, an initiative that gives drug offenders the choice to enter substance abuse rehabilitation programs instead of prison. Many drug reform supporters are calling the proposition a success. A similar initiative, Proposition 36, was passed four years later in California.

Many experts applaud the shifting approach in the war on drugs and claim that alternative sanctions can offer potential solutions to the challenges posed by drug abuse and the overburdened prison system. For instance, proponents of alternative sanctions contend that sending drug offenders to treatment can alleviate taxpayers of the skyrocketing costs of corrections. Although residential treatment for a drug addict can cost up to $7,000 a year, the annual cost of incarceration starts at $25,000. Advocates also assert that diverting drug offenders from the prison system will enhance public safety in two ways. First, it will make more prison space available to incapacitate violent offenders and career criminals. Second, because many drug addicts commit crimes such as theft and prostitution in order to pay for their drug habits, ending drug offenders' addictions can lower the crime rate. A State of Connecticut report claims that alternatives to incarceration are two to five times more effective than prison in lowering drug crimes.

However, detractors of initiatives such as Propositions 36 and 200 claim that incarceration is necessary to treat drug offenders. Criminal justice investigator David Cole suggests that the "introduction of judicial authority and criminal sanctions appears to make treatment more effective." Proposition 36 has even been criticized by former drug addicts and alcoholics. Actor Martin Sheen, who successfully recovered from alcoholism, says the initiative "takes away the leverage that a judge has to get an addict's attention." Some experts maintain that Proposition 36 is too lenient and may actually keep more drug offenders on the streets than in treatment. According to an analysis of Proposition 36 by the Rand Corporation, "Probation caseloads are very high. A person who quits a treatment program is unlikely to draw the same kind of attention as a violent offender who does not meet his or her conditions."

Some opponents argue that alternative sanctions such as drug treatment unfairly favor offenders belonging to the middle and upper classes. They claim that most drug offenders from the lower class are unable to afford drug treatment and end up in prison. According to Corey Pearson, a former volunteer with the Prisoners' Rights Union, "The programs which work are usually reserved for populations which have the means to avoid falling into the criminal justice system abyss—generally the middle class."

Other critics maintain that drug treatment is plainly ineffective and should not be used as an alternative to incarceration. For example, former federal drug policy directors William J. Bennett and John P. Walters insist that "overall, cocaine treatment is only 4 percent effective in reducing heavy use and 2 percent more effective in reducing heavy use than no treatment at all." They also criticize drug courts and alternative sanctions for drug offenders, contending that "a very large number of addicted offenders today are long-term, hard-core addicts who are poorly suited for diversion programs."

Proponents of alternative sanctions contend that sentencing drug offenders to treatment instead of prison can more effectively supervise the ever-growing numbers of drug abusers caught in the net of the justice system. They insist that drug treatment is more beneficial than incarceration because it is more economical and promotes public safety by lowering recidivism rates and keeping dangerous criminals behind bars. Yet opponents argue that removing incarceration from the drug treatment equation eliminates a powerful incentive for drug offenders to change their ways. They also maintain that initiatives such as Proposition 36 will cast drug abusers out of supervision into the grip of addiction. *America's Prisons: Opposing Viewpoints* investigates this dilemma and other challenges facing America's prisons in the following chapters: Are Prisons Effective? How Should Prisons Treat Inmates? Should Prisons Use Inmate Labor? What Are the Alternatives to Prisons? These chapters explore the major arguments shaping the future of America's prison system.

CHAPTER 1

Are Prisons Effective?

Chapter Preface

Studies report that 1 million African Americans account for half of the U.S. prison population, while 70 percent of the prison population are people of color. Meanwhile, white Americans comprise 70 percent of the general U.S. population.

Many critics assert that these statistics are the results of a racist criminal justice system. They argue that blacks are seven times more likely to be imprisoned than whites, at a rate of 700 per 100,000. Critics also add that the war on drugs is racially biased and responsible for the growing racial disparity in prisons. According to prison reform activist Pamela Davis, "People of color are subject to far more intense modes of surveillance than white people. . . . Although the rate of illicit drug use among white people is actually greater than blacks, black people are arrested and convicted on drug charges far more frequently."

Supporters of the criminal justice system dispute allegations that it enforces racist policies. U.S. Justice Department statistician Patrick A. Langan admits that racism has troubled the criminal justice system in previous decades, but he insists that contemporary "studies exist showing no bias in arrest, prosecution, adjudication, and sentencing." For instance, Langan claims that in one study "the average state prison sentence received by blacks convicted of a felony was five and one-half years. That is one month longer than what whites received, a small difference not of statistical significance."

Whether or not the justice system is racist is one of the debates that emerges in discussions of the effectiveness of prisons. In the following chapter, authors present their views on whether the right people are put behind bars and whether the American public is safer for it.

"Although the cost of building and maintaining more prisons is high, the cost of not doing so appears to be higher."

The Prison System Works

Peter du Pont

In the following viewpoint, Peter du Pont claims that the prison system works. Since the probability of being imprisoned for committing a crime has increased, he contends, crimes such as rape and murder have been reduced. According to du Pont, the enormous cost of imprisoning more criminals pays for itself by preventing future crimes and increasing public safety. He also asserts that these costs can be reduced through reforms of the prison system. Du Pont is a former governor of Delaware and the policy chairman for the National Center for Policy analysis, a nonprofit, nonpartisan think tank based in Texas.

As you read, consider the following questions:
1. How does the author support his claim that the increased probability of imprisonment reduces crime?
2. According to du Pont, how much money is saved as the "social benefit" from imprisoning an offender?
3. Why does du Pont support inmate labor?

Reprinted from "Winning the War Against Criminals," by Peter du Pont, *The San Diego Union-Tribune*, September 11, 1998. Reprinted with permission from the author.

Who's winning lately, the cops or the crooks? Fortunately, law enforcement is, and that means we're all safer.

The improvements in daily living are pretty obvious in our great cities, and even in depressed neighborhoods, chaos, crime and open-air drug markets are in retreat. Talk about improving the environment! Real jobs, coherent family living and civilization itself depend on a tolerable degree of protection of life and property. And the thin blue line has been working lately.

Encouraging Trends

Nationally, the overall rate of serious crime is at a 25-year low [in 1998]. The murder rate is lower than in the 1970s. In New York City, it is as low as in the 1960s. The FBI's crime statistics show that every category of violent crime has decreased since 1993.

A major reason for the one-third crime slide during the 1990s is that crime has become more expensive for adult perpetrators. The likelihood of serving prison time for committing a serious violent crime or a burglary has increased substantially.

According to a study from the National Center for Policy Analysis, murder has dropped 30 percent as the probability of going to prison for murder has risen 53 percent. Rape has decreased 14 percent as the probability of imprisonment has increased 12 percent; robbery has decreased 29 percent as the probability of imprisonment has increased 28 percent; burglary has decreased 18 percent as the probability of imprisonment has increased 14 percent.

Moreover, once in prison, criminals are staying there longer. The median time served by those released recently has risen since 1993 for every major category except aggravated assault.

Are these trends related? Common sense says yes, even if sociologists continue to deny it. Criminals choose whether to commit specific crimes or not, and they've decided on fewer crimes, a pretty rational response.

Meanwhile, the prison and jail population has doubled since the mid-1980s to 1.8 million. Nobody's really happy about this but at least the expense has improved public safety. We now spend $120 billion a year on the justice system, or, over $1,000 in taxes per household each year. If we're going to further depress the crime rate, the justice system has to make crime even less profitable by further increases in expected punishment. Unfortunately, that means more prison beds.

Prisons Do Not Create Criminals

We hear all the time that prisons create crime—that imprisonment turns first-time offenders into hardened criminals. If this argument were true, then [another] proposition would have to be true as well: that many offenders sentenced to prison are not already hardened criminals, . . .

So-called "first-offenders" are often nothing of the sort. In some cases, "first-offenders" have lengthy juvenile records that are unavailable by law to the adult criminal justice system. These "first-offenders" are already hardened criminals. In other cases, offenders get probation for their first adult offense, and sometimes even for subsequent offenses committed while on probation. . . . Former Attorney General Hal Stratton of New Mexico has summed it up: "I don't know anyone that goes to prison on their first crime. By the time you go to prison, you are a pretty bad guy."

U.S. Department of Justice, *The Case for More Incarceration*, 1992.

But a tough approach pays, especially over the long run. As the odds worsen for criminals, crime declines and the same number of arrests and convictions further raise the odds against criminals.

Although the cost of building and maintaining more prisons is high, the cost of not doing so appears to be higher. One study found that each additional prisoner reduces the number of non-drug crimes by approximately 15 per year, a social benefit of $53,000 annually, or more. Even at $25,000 to $30,000 a year, the taxpayers' cost of keeping the average criminal locked up is worthwhile.

Cost Saving Options

The annual cost of lock-ups can be reduced by more competition in their supply. A handful of academic studies shows that private prisons save taxpayers money while providing superior performance in almost every way, including lower recidivism among inmates released from private facilities.

[Another] option, yet untested, is to contract out to non-profit groups, including faith-based prison operators. As professor Richard Moran of Holyoke College says, "A private, not-for-profit foundation is in the best position to organize a prison around a set of principles intended to reshape criminals into honest, productive citizens." Despite our lack of a "model" or successful prison, no jurisdiction or politician has yet had the courage or good sense to try something new in jail suppliers, despite the obvious successes non-governmental and faith-based hospitals, schools and juvenile programs have had.

Another cost saver would be to engage prisoners in productive work so that they pay more of their own way, repay victims and support their own families. Prisons today reek of idleness. The only way to get prisoners off welfare on a mass basis is to recruit the private sector. Prison-run work programs have been failures. Our aim should be to propel offenders into, rather than away from, successful participation in the labor force.

Rep. Bill McCollum, R-Fla., chairman of the House Judiciary's crime committee, says, "We can't overemphasize how important this is," and he recently introduced H.R. 4100, the so-called Free Market Prison Industries Reform Act of 1998 [which did not pass], to make it easier to hire prisoners. It would repeal the federal law which bans interstate commerce in prison-made goods and switch the Federal Prison Industries from its socialist format to private production for the open market. Its passage would be a wonderful step toward rationality in our prison policies.

> *"The system we have designed to deal with offenders is . . . nurturing those very qualities it claims to deter."*

The Prison System Does Not Work

Jerome Miller

Jerome Miller is the founder and executive director of the National Center for Institutions and Alternatives, an organization that develops alternatives to imprisonment and seeks solutions to prison overcrowding. In the following viewpoint, Miller contends that the prison system does not work because it unfairly incarcerates minorities and perpetuates antisocial behavior by treating them inhumanely. The public's "vicious" mood towards crime, Miller suggests, influences politicians to devise increasingly punitive criminal justice policies for an already overburdened and violent prison system.

As you read, consider the following questions:
1. What example does the author use to support his view that the criminal-justice system unfairly incarcerates African Americans for drug offenses?
2. What are Miller's three leading causes of prison overcrowding?
3. According to Miller, how does the prison system exacerbate violent behavior?

Excerpted from "American Gulag," by Jerome Miller, *Yes! A Journal of Positive Futures*, Fall 2000. Reprinted with permission from *Yes!*, PO Box 10818, Bainbridge Island, WA 98110. For subscriptions call 1-800-937-4451 or visit www.yesmagazine.org.

The figures are startling. In the last year of the Carter administration (1979), our nation's federal prisons held about 20,000 inmates. By contrast, as the Clinton administration draws to a close we will have 135,000 inmates in federal prisons; projecting an annual growth of 10 percent the number will reach a quarter million in five years. In 1979, there were 268,000 inmates in the prisons of all 50 states. Today, they hold almost 1.3 million. In 1979, there were 150,000 in local jails and lockups. Today, local jail facilities hold nearly 700,000. In 2000, we will exceed 2 million inmates in our prisons and jails. As we enter the millennium, the nation has about 6.5 million of its citizens under some form of correctional supervision.

And a new twist has been added: the "supermax" prison composed exclusively of cells used for solitary confinement. A place of studied sensual deprivation and psychological torture, it was designed by correctional managers to control their populations as privileges in routine prisons were diminished and sentences were lengthened. A product less of management necessity than of a twisted psyche, these temples to sado-masochism now dot the American landscape, presently containing 20,000 mostly minority inmates.

Astonishing Patterns of Racial Bias

Spurred on by a "drug war" that focuses inordinately upon the poor and minorities, we have seen astonishing patterns of incarceration among young black men vis à vis similarly accused white men. Although the rates of drug consumption are roughly equal among white and black populations, blacks are imprisoned for drug offenses at 14 times the rate of whites.

The patterns in some states are truly astonishing. Between 1986 and 1996 for example, the rate of incarceration for drug offenses among African Americans increased by 10,102 percent in Louisiana; in Georgia, by 5,499 percent; in Arkansas 5,033 percent; in Iowa 4,284 percent; and in Tennessee 1,473 percent.

There are currently more than 50 million criminal records on file in the US, with at least 4 to 5 million "new" adults acquiring such a record annually. This record sticks with a person, whether or not charges are dropped or there is a subsequent conviction. A notorious example occurred in the recent police killing of Patrick Dorismond, an unarmed young Haitian immigrant. In an attempt to rationalize the police behavior, Mayor Rudolph Giuliani characterized the deceased as "no altar boy" and released a "criminal record" that included two past convictions for "disorderly conduct" and a juvenile charge that had been dismissed over two decades earlier when Dorismond was 13 years old.

For certain racial and ethnic groups, being arrested and locked up is a given. Beginning in adolescence, we have established a warped "rite of passage" for young African Americans and Hispanics; only by a fluke will they avoid acquiring a "criminal record"—the result of an arrest.

In 1990, the nonprofit Washington, DC–based Sentencing Project found that on an average day, one in every four African-American men ages 20–29 was either in prison, in jail, or on probation/parole. Ten years later, the ratio had shrunk to one in three.

Research conducted by the National Center on Institutions and Alternatives revealed that more than half of young black males living in Washington, DC, and Baltimore are caught up in the criminal justice system on an average day— either in prison, jail, on probation or parole, out on bond, or being sought on a warrant.

Three of every four (76 percent) African-American 18-year-olds living in urban areas can now anticipate being arrested and jailed before age 36. In the process, each young man will acquire a "criminal record." By the late 1990s, federal statisticians were predicting that nearly one of every three adult black men in the nation could anticipate being sentenced to a federal or state prison at some time during his life. . . .

The uncomfortable truth is that the national attitude on crime is more firmly grounded in race than in putative crime rates. The surge in crime rates occurred between 1965 and 1973. The general trend since that time, with "blips" in 1989 and 1991, has been for crime to either remain stable or to decline.

While most people assume jail overcrowding results from rising crime rates, increased violence, or general population growth, that is seldom the case. Here, in order of importance, are the major contributors to jail overcrowding:

1. The number of police officers
2. The number of judges
3. The number of courtrooms
4. The size of the district attorney's staff
5. Policies of the state's attorney's office concerning which crimes deserve the most attention
6. The size of the staff of the entire court system
7. The number of beds available in the local jail
8. The willingness of victims to report crimes
9. Police department policies concerning arrest
10. The arrest rate within the police department
11. The actual amount of crime committed

It is common for a "trickle-up effect" to set in. Although there may be little or no change in the ways serious crimes are handled, those who engage in minor infractions of the law end up receiving harsh penalties as well, thereby "casting the net" of social control ever wider. Such matters should give the nation pause as we move aggressively to build more prisons and camps, but there is little to suggest any respite.

The distinguished British criminologist Andrew Rutherford summarized the trend well: "All natural tendencies toward stability appear to have evaporated. Not only has there been a quantum leap of unprecedented proportions in prison populations, but there appear also to be no indications of any counter forces which might impose limits."

Carnegie-Mellon criminologist Alfred Blumstein put it another way: "Once criminal policy in the United States fell into the political arena, little could be done to recapture concern for limiting prison populations. . . . Our political system learned an overly simplistic trick: when it responds to such pressures by sternly demanding increased punishments, that approach has been found to be strikingly effective, not in solving the problem, but in alleviating the political pressure to 'do something.'"

The Signs of a Society in Danger

To many, the "tough on crime" attitude seems a good thing— a return to basic values, a focus on the rights of victims, an adieu to the "bleeding heart" policies of the past. Overall, the prevailing public mood on crime is vicious.

I recently watched a video of a "focus group" on crime conducted by a Republican pollster and consultant. In discussing a recent shooting of a teacher by a 13-year-old African-American middle-school honor student, the consultant asked the group what they would do in such a case. Their response seemed even to embarrass him as he tried to smile away the comments of this scientifically chosen "average" group of local citizens. "Fry him!" came the insistent shouts from the group as the 13-year-old's situation was being presented. Only one older African-American man remained silent. . . .

Indeed, prisons and jails are an "early warning system" of

One sign of a criminal justice system in trouble

Leigh Rubin. Reprinted with permission from Creators Syndicate.

sorts for a society. They constitute the canary in the coal mine, providing an omen of mortal danger that often lies beyond our capacity to perceive.

The experience of the past two decades suggests that we are ignoring this warning. We are in a curious position in which a surfeit of prisons filled with a million minority young men is seen not as an embarrassment, but as indispensable to the smooth running of our democracy and integral to its economy. In effect, the attitude that suffused Southern jails and prisons during post–Civil War reconstruction has been replicated nationally.

For more than 20 years, our politicians have played the dangerous game of one-upping each other over who can demand the harshest punishments. In this pursuit, the definition of what is criminal, the relaxing of limits on the police to enforce laws, and the mandatory use of prison over non-institutional means of control or correction have been distilled to carefully crafted marketing slogans like "three strikes and you're out."

A Warped Conception

Offenders emerge from prison afraid to trust, fearful of the unknown, and with a vision of the world shaped by the meaning that behaviors had in the prison context. For a recently released prisoner, experiences like being jostled on the subway, having someone reach across him in the bathroom to take a paper towel, or making eye contact can be taken as a precursor to a physical attack. In relationships with loved ones, this warped kind of socialization means that problems will not easily be talked through. In a sense, the system we have designed to deal with offenders is among the most iatrogenic in history, nurturing those very qualities it claims to deter. . . .

I vividly remember the case of Doug, a stocky 16-year-old addicted to heroin. Late one evening, returning home from a meeting near the state reform school over which I'd recently assumed control, I decided to take a quick side trip to the so-called disciplinary cottage. I asked the "master" on duty whether anyone was upstairs in the "tombs," (the strip cells that I'd ordered closed a few weeks earlier). No. I guess he thought I wouldn't bother to go upstairs and look. There, in a far corner of one of the dim cells, was Doug, lying stripped on the bare cement floor. I stood in the doorway trying to talk through the mesh security screen that separated us. "How long have you been here?" The muffled reply: "A few days." "Why are you here?" His voice grew more agitated: "I tried to make it over the fence out back." I told him I wanted him to come out and go back downstairs. "We aren't using the tombs anymore." Doug let go a torrent of obscenities—"You naïve asshole! You dumb motherfucker! Don't you know kids like me need to be in here?"

Doug had learned his lessons well. He had become the well-socialized product of our reform school—a "disciplinary cottage success" who believed what it taught. The way to handle unacceptable impulses is to be grabbed, beaten, handcuffed, dragged screaming up cement steps, stripped, and thrown into a "tomb."

It's not that we don't know that our present medieval tapestry of crime and punishment will at some point unravel. It isn't that there aren't alternative ways presently available for dealing with those who threaten us or break our laws. However, at times they seem largely futile, if not actually counter-productive. In the present poisoned atmosphere, even the most well-intentioned alternatives run the danger of being pummeled to serve the very same warped conception of humanity they would challenge.

Somewhere in my youth I learned that the only unforgivable sin is the sin of despair. For that reason if no other, I choose to continue what has become a somewhat melancholy battle. It is a great comfort to know that so many others continue to exercise their hope for a better way with equanimity and crazy joy.

"[Prison] is not the whole solution, but it is the first essential step in ridding America of the menace of violent crime."

More Imprisonment Is Needed

Patrick F. Fagan and Robert E. Moffit

An individual who engages in habitual criminal activity is referred to as a "hardcore criminal" or "repeat offender." In the following viewpoint, Patrick F. Fagan and Robert E. Moffit assert that this minority of criminals commit the majority of violent crimes and that more imprisonment is needed to incapacitate them. Pretrial release, probation, parole, and "light sentencing," according to Fagan and Moffit, often release repeat offenders into communities, resulting in more violent crime and endangering public safety. The authors suggest that these programs be sharply restricted and that prison space be expanded to accommodate more convicts. Fagan is a William H.G. FitzGerald Senior Fellow at the Heritage Foundation, where Moffit is the director of Domestic Policy Issues. The Heritage Foundation is a non-profit conservative policy think tank.

As you read, consider the following questions:
1. According to Fagan and Moffit, what is the leading cause of crime?
2. How do Fagan and Moffit support their claim that repeat offenders commit most violent crimes?
3. Why is pretrial release dangerous as stated by the authors?

Excerpted from "Chapter 8 Crime," by Patrick F. Fagan and Robert E. Moffit, *Issues '96: The Candidate's Briefing Book*, 1996. Reprinted with permission from the Heritage Foundation. Article available at www.heritagefoundation.org/issues/96/chpt8.html.

On October 15, 1995, Senator Barbara Mikulski was mugged outside her home in Baltimore. Robert Eugene Perlie, charged with the crime, was on probation for possession of cocaine and resisting arrest. He also had been convicted in the past for other drug offenses, as well as for theft and insurance fraud. Moreover, at the time of the incident, Perlie was scheduled for four separate trials on charges of illegal transportation of a handgun, violation of probation, drug possession, and malicious destruction and theft.

The Mikulski mugging represents in microcosm both the problem and the politics of crime in America: A relatively small, hard-core group of repeat offenders commit most crimes, especially violent crimes. Federal lawmakers talk about "getting tough on crime" and then pass laws that affect only the tiny minority of hard-core criminals that come under federal jurisdiction, leaving the vast majority unaffected. Press releases tout federal efforts, even though career criminals remain on the streets. The public becomes more cynical and more alarmed.

The Essential First Step

Conservative candidates should explain the short-term solution to America's crime problem: putting repeat offenders behind bars and keeping them there. This is not the whole solution, but it is the essential first step in ridding America of the menace of violent crime. And the evidence shows that it works. This means, however, that federal lawmakers must stop posturing for the cameras and recognize that, because most violent street crime is under the jurisdiction of state and local governments, most of the changes in policy need to be made at the state and local levels. . . .

In the long term, lawmakers at all levels must recognize that the real reason for America's decades-long crime wave is not poverty, as some have believed. Nor is it race, as others have intimated. It is family breakdown. Nothing could be clearer from the social research than that fatherless children from whatever socioeconomic or racial background are the most likely to commit violent crimes as teenagers and adults. The rising rate of illegitimacy means that teenage crime also will continue to rise. This point must be driven home, repeatedly, and long-range economic and social policies that encourage the formation of stable, two-parent families must be developed. At the same time, Americans must face the fact that some existing government policies encourage illegitimacy and family breakup. To curb crime, these anti-family policies must be ended. . . .

While crime rates have declined somewhat [in 1995], they are still very high compared with 1960. In 1960, there were 160 violent crimes for every 100,000 Americans; by 1994, there were 715 for every 100,000 Americans, down slightly from 1993. Overall, there were 23,310 murders, 102,100 rapes, 618,820 robberies, and 1,119,950 aggravated assaults in 1994. Since 1990, violent and property crime have declined by 2.2 percent and 8.5 percent respectively, per 100,000 inhabitants.

While still devastating in its impact on American society, the recent downturn is both welcome and, according to John DiIulio, Professor of Politics and Public Affairs at Princeton University, "can be explained in part by policy-driven law enforcement efforts that capitalize on community crime-fighting initiatives and take the bad guys off the streets."

Conservatives therefore should welcome the debate over crime. Liberals, on the other hand, continue to look to social programs to reduce crime even though these programs have proved ineffective. The fact is that recent success in reducing crime is largely attributable to conservative policies which emphasize tougher and more effective law enforcement and incarceration of violent criminals. Crime is still a politically powerful issue throughout the nation, and in few areas are the political lines clearer. The American people have had enough; they are demanding tough, sweeping changes that will slash the crime rate.

The effectiveness of good police work and extended incarceration of hardened criminals is beyond dispute. Crime rates would drop even more dramatically if more state and local officials initiated tougher and more effective law enforcement on America's streets, as Professor DiIulio suggests, and made violent criminals serve longer prison terms. . . .

Crime and Family Breakdown

The insufficiency or absence of government social programs does not fuel violent crime. The social science literature is conclusive on one all-important point: The real root cause of violent crime is the breakdown of family and community, especially in America's inner cities.

The professional literature shows that the failure of fathers and mothers to care for the children they bring into the world is at the heart of violent crime. Absent fathers, absent mothers, parental fighting and domestic violence, lack of parental supervision and discipline of children, patterns of parental abuse, neglect or rejection of the child, and criminality among the parents themselves all are conditions that contribute to the creation of a violent criminal, and all are most present in the social atmosphere created by broken families and illegitimacy.

Crime and Race

While serious crime is highest in socially disorganized, largely urban neighborhoods, however, its frequency is not a function of race. The determining factor is the absence of marriage. Among broken families, with their chaotic, "dysfunctional" relationships, whether white or black, the crime rate is very high; among married, two-parent families, whether white or black, the crime rate is very low. The capacity and determination to maintain stable married relationships, not race, is the pivotal factor. The chaotic, broken community stems from these chaotic, broken families. The reason race appears to be an important factor in crime is the prevalence of wide differences in marriage rates among ethnic groups. A report from the state of Wisconsin further illustrates this.

Between 1980 and 1993, according to the latest available data, the number of black inmates rose from 46.5 percent to 50.8 percent of the total prison population, from 140,600 to 445,400. Justice Department findings show that, at the end of 1993, blacks were seven times more likely than whites to have been incarcerated in a state or federal prison. An estimated 1,471 blacks per 100,000 black residents and 207 whites per 100,000 white residents were incarcerated in the nation's prisons on December 31, 1993.

The fact that crime rates are much higher for blacks than whites has tempted some to cite race as a factor in overall crime. It is therefore important for candidates to explain that the evidence does not support this view. When social scientists control for family structure, the rates for blacks and whites are not significantly different. Broken families are most closely correlated with violent crime, regardless of race. In other words, family structure, not race, is the leading indicator of criminal behavior. There is a higher rate of crime among blacks only because black communities have higher rates of illegitimacy and family breakup.

Public Enemy No. 1: The Repeat Offender

Study after study shows that habitual offenders, who amount to a tiny fraction of the total population, commit most violent crimes.

- A February 1992 follow-up for the 1983 special report on recidivism, the nation's largest survey of felons on probation showed that of the 79,000 felons released from prison in 32 counties across 17 states in 1986, an estimated 43 percent, while out on probation, were re-arrested for a felony or misdemeanor within three years. Half of these arrests were for violent crimes or drug offenses. Within three years of their release, 54 percent had one or more arrests, 24 percent had two or more, and the remaining 22 percent had 3 or more. Also within three years of release, 46 percent of all probationers had been sent back to prison or jail. The study showed that of the 79,043 former prisoners on probation, 43 percent (34,000), were re-arrested and charged with a felony 64,000 times during the three-year follow-up period. . . .
- A RAND study found that 76 percent of former prison inmates in California were re-arrested within three years of release and that 60 percent were convicted of new crimes. In Texas, 60 percent of former inmates were re-arrested within three years of release, and 40 percent were re-convicted within this time.
- A 1992 study by the Bureau of Alcohol, Tobacco, and Firearms found that the average criminal serving time for firearms offenses commits 160 crimes per year before being incarcerated. . . .

The Danger of Pretrial Release

Too many hard-core repeat offenders commit crimes while out on bail pending trial on previous criminal charges.

The Bureau of Justice Statistics reports that one in six felony defendants in 1988 was re-arrested on new felony charges while out on bail pending trial. Some 30 percent of felony defendants with five or more prior convictions and out on bail pending trial were re-arrested during 1988; incredibly, two-thirds of these re-arrested defendants were released again pending trial on the new charges.

A study of pretrial release in 75 of the nation's most populous counties found that 18 percent of felony defendants in 1988 were re-arrested for new felonies while out on bail pending trial. Again, two-thirds were released on bail while awaiting trial on these new charges.

Locking Up Career Criminals

The vast majority of inmates are career criminals, as demonstrated in Arizona, where in 1996 voters approved a drug-liberalization ballot initiative. The initiative would have required the release of all inmates sentenced for first-time drug offenses—about 1,000 inmates in all. But in 1997, the state legislature amended the law to disqualify from this amnesty all first-time drug inmates previously convicted of a felony. As a result, the number of inmates entitled to freedom shrank to 53. Americans clearly are locking up the right people.

Andrew Peyton Thomas, *The Weekly Standard*, November 30, 1998.

The kind of outrage that can result from lax pretrial policies is exemplified by the case of Hernando Williams, an Illinois criminal defendant released pending trial on charges of aggravated kidnapping, rape, and armed robbery. While awaiting trial, he kidnapped and raped another woman and locked her in the trunk of his car for several days. He showed up for his court appearance with the woman still locked in the trunk of his car. After that appearance, he committed further sexual assaults on this second victim and then shot and killed her. . . .

How Criminals Have Been Kept out of Jail

During the 1960s, crime policies based on liberal theories of social injustice sent fewer criminals to prison for shorter terms. The number of offenders imprisoned for every 1,000 violent crime arrests plummeted by almost 50 percent, from 299 in 1960 to 170 in 1970. Tougher law-enforcement policies began to return in the 1970s, and the crime rate slowed as the rate of incarceration increased 38 percent. In the conservative 1980s, far tougher policies were adopted.

According to the Bureau of Justice Statistics, on December 31, 1994, the number of sentenced prisoners per 100,000 U.S. residents was 387 up from 139 in 1980. The rate of incarceration more than doubled from 1980 to 1990, increasing by 219 percent. In 1980, there were 329,821 federal and state prisoners; by 1990, there were 773,919. By 1994, the total number of people incarcerated in federal and state penitentiaries since 1980 had increased 219 percent to 1,053,738.

Conservative candidates should note the correlation: With more violent repeat offenders locked up in prison, and therefore unable to commit crimes against the public, the result has been the reduction in serious crime rates noted earlier.

The Failure and Abuse of Probation and Parole

Liberals in Congress and elsewhere often bemoan the fact that there are more than 5 million persons in the United States under "correctional supervision." While it is true that the U.S. prison population is at an all-time high, however, most of those incarcerated are violent criminals or repeat offenders. Moreover, while approximately 1 million persons are imprisoned, an overwhelming majority of convicts, another 3.5 million, or 72 percent are not in prison, but on probation or parole, and the disparity between the rate of imprisonment and the rate of release on probation or parole has been growing in recent years. Between 1980 and 1994, while the prison population increased by 184 percent, the parole and probation population increased by 204 percent.

A large proportion of America's crime problem derives from the fact that so many criminals, including violent and repeat offenders, are out on the streets. According to Professor DiIulio, nearly one-third of parolees imprisoned for violent crimes, and nearly one-fifth of those imprisoned for a crime against property, are re-arrested within three years of their release for committing a violent crime. Among convicted felons on probation alone, 54 percent are arrested once, 24 percent are arrested twice, and 22 percent are arrested three or more times. . . .

How Light Prison Sentences and Parole Lead to Crime

Another problem is that criminals generally serve only a fraction of their sentences, even as sentences themselves are often too short.

Because of parole and early release programs, sentences handed down by state courts do not indicate time actually served. . . .

Data collected from the states by the Bureau of Justice Statistics indicate that for violent crimes, the average time served is three years and seven months (43 months) or 48 percent of the original sentence (89 months). For murder, the average is only five years and 11 months (71 months) or 48 percent of the original sentence (149 months); for robbery, three years and eight months (44 months) or 46 percent of the original sentence (95 months); and for rape, five years and five months (65 months) or 56 percent of the original sentence (117 months).

These short prison terms for violent repeat offenders do more than trigger a sense of injustice among victims. They also mean more crime. . . .

What Should Be Done

Sharply restrict pre-trial release for dangerous defendants. States should enact legislation and, if necessary, amend their constitutions to allow for detention without bail pending trial for defendants who pose a proven threat to victims, witnesses, or the community at large. Legislation to grant judges this power in federal courts was adopted in 1984. Under this law, a judge who finds that release will endanger the safety of any other person or the community, and that no combination of conditions on a release can reasonably assure such safety, may deny bail and order the defendant detained until trial. Any defendant convicted within the past five years of a violent crime committed on pre-trial release is automatically presumed to be a danger to the community. An additional sentence of two to 10 years also applies to any felony committed while on pre-trial release.

This law has worked well at the federal level and provides a model that should be adopted by every state to prevent repeat offenders from committing crimes pending trial, which remains a significant problem.

Sharply limit probation. Probation should be prohibited for the following serious offenses: murder, rape, armed robbery, felonies involving the intentional or knowing infliction of serious physical injury, or a second conviction for any felony. Probation leaves these classes of criminals free to threaten law-abiding citizens. Limiting it is a commonsense way to keep serious repeat offenders off the streets.

Adopt strict state sentencing guidelines. A comprehensive and complex set of guidelines developed by the U.S. Sentencing Commission has been adopted to govern sentencing for federal crimes. These guidelines specify a narrow range of sentences for each crime which vary according to the seriousness of the crime, the prior record of the defendant, whether a weapon was used, how much bodily injury or financial loss was caused, and other factors. Federal judges must impose sentences within this narrow range, except in cases where the judge believes special circumstances warrant a departure. The prosecution or defense may appeal a sentence departing from the guidelines, and such departure will not be upheld without a strong and valid justification.

If states adopted such sentencing guidelines, liberal or lenient judges would be hard pressed to evade them. This is one of the most important reforms state officials could adopt to get repeat offenders off the streets.

Abolish parole for violent offenders. Under federal sentencing guidelines, parole has been all but abolished. Early release is allowed only for "good time credits," which may reduce the imposed sentence by no more than 15 percent. If states adopted this standard, it could be a powerful weapon in the fight to keep violent repeat offenders in prison. Virginia Governor George Allen made this reform a central theme in his criminal justice reform program.

Acquire adequate prison space. No reform aimed at incarcerating repeat and violent criminals can succeed without sufficient prison space. In most jurisdictions, including the federal system, this means constructing or otherwise acquiring additional capacity. As former Attorney General Barr has said, "The choice is clear: More prison space or more crime."

Lawmakers can justify this expenditure by noting that the cost of acquiring additional prison space is offset not only by the far larger savings to society from reducing crime, but also by the incalculable benefits derived from protecting the lives and property of American citizens.

"Prisons became, in a very real sense, a substitute for the more constructive social policies we were avoiding."

More Imprisonment Is Not Needed

Elliot Currie

In the following viewpoint, Elliot Currie contends that the drastic increases in the imprisonment rate during the past twenty-five years have done little to reduce crime. Imprisonment has become the "default solution" for America's social problems such as poverty and mental illness, Currie argues, and has taken the place of social programs that can help to reduce crime, such as child welfare and job training services. He also asserts that the slashing of federal spending from social programs for the poor mirrors budget increases for prisons, which entrap the lower classes in a continuing cycle of crime, poverty, and family instability. Currie, a criminologist, has written several books on crime and teaches in the Legal Studies Program at the University of California at Berkeley.

As you read, consider the following questions:
1. According to the author, how much higher is America's imprisonment rate compared to similar countries?
2. How does Currie support his claim that the drop in crime has not been experienced in all of America's major cities?
3. In Currie's opinion, the prison system has become the "substitute" for which social policies?

Just as violent crime has become part of the accepted backdrop of life in the United States, so too has the growth of the system we've established to contain it. A huge and constantly expanding penal system seems to us like a normal and inevitable feature of modern life. But what we have witnessed in the past quarter century is nothing less than a revolution in our justice system—a transformation unprecedented in our own history, or in that of any other industrial democracy.

The Prison Explosion

In 1971 there were fewer than 200,000 inmates in our state and federal prisons. By the end of 1996 we were approaching 1.2 million. The prison population, in short, has nearly sextupled in the course of twenty-five years. Adding in local jails brings the total to nearly 1.7 million. To put the figure of 1.7 million into perspective, consider that it is roughly equal to the population of Houston, Texas, the fourth-largest city in the nation, and more than twice that of San Francisco. Our overall national population has grown, too, of course, but the prison population has grown much faster: as a *proportion* of the American population, the number behind bars has more than quadrupled. During the entire period from the end of World War II to the early 1970s, the nation's prison incarceration rate—the number of inmates in state and federal prisons per 100,000 population—fluctuated in a narrow band between a low of 93 (in 1972) and a high of 119 (in 1961). By 1996 it had reached 427 per 100,000. . . .

The effect of this explosion on some communities is by now well known, thanks to the work of the Washington-based Sentencing Project, the Center on Juvenile and Criminal Justice in San Francisco, and others. By the mid-1990s roughly one in three young black men were under the "supervision" of the criminal justice system—that is, in a jail or prison, on probation or parole, or under pretrial release. The figure was two out of five in California, and over half in the city of Baltimore, Maryland. In California today, four times as many black men are "enrolled" in state prison as are enrolled in public colleges and universities. Nationally, there are twice as many black men in state and federal prison today as there were men of all races twenty years ago. More than anything else, it is the war on drugs that has caused this dramatic increase: between 1985 and 1995, the number of black state prison inmates sentenced for drug offenses rose by more than 700 percent. Less discussed, but even more startling, is the enormous increase in the number of Hispanic prisoners, which has more than quintupled since 1980 alone. . . .

A Punitive Country

Seen in the context of a single country, even these extraordinary figures on the "boom" in imprisonment lose meaning. But when we place the American experience in international perspective its uniqueness becomes clear. The simplest way to do this is to compare different countries' incarceration rates—the number of people behind bars as a proportion of the population. In 1995, the most recent year we can use for comparative purposes, the overall incarceration rate for the United States was 600 per 100,000 population, including local jails (but not juvenile institutions). Around the world, the only country with a higher rate was Russia, at 690 per 100,000. Several other countries of the former Soviet bloc also had high rates—270 per 100,000 in Estonia, for example, and 200 in Romania—as did, among others, Singapore (229) and South Africa (368). But most industrial democracies clustered *far* below us, at around 55 to 120 per 100,000, with a few—notably Japan, at 36—lower still. Spain and the United Kingdom, our closest "competitors" among the major nations of western Europe, imprison their citizens at a rate roughly one-sixth of ours; Holland and Scandinavia, about one-tenth. . . .

No matter how we approach the question, then, the United States *does* turn out to be relatively punitive in its treatment of offenders, and very much so for less serious crimes. Yet in an important sense, this way of looking at the issue of "punitiveness" sidesteps the deeper implications of the huge international differences in incarceration. For it is arguably the incarceration rate itself, not the rate per offense, that tells us the most important things about a nation's approach to crime and punishment. An incarceration rate that is many times higher than that of comparable countries is a signal that something is very wrong. Either the country

43

is punishing offenders with a severity far in excess of what is considered normal in otherwise similar societies, or it is breeding a far higher level of serious crime, or both. In the case of the U.S., it is indeed both. The evidence suggests that we are more punitive when it comes to property and drug crimes, but not as far from the norm in punishing violent crimes. We have an unusually high incarceration rate, then, partly because of our relatively punitive approach to nonviolent offenses, and partly because of our high level of serious violent crime. On both counts, the fact that we imprison our population at a rate six to ten times higher than that of other advanced societies means that we rely far more on our penal system to maintain social order—to enforce the rules of our common social life—than other industrial nations do. In a very real sense, we have been engaged in an experiment, testing the degree to which a modern industrial society can maintain public order through the threat of punishment. That is the more profound meaning of the charge that America is an unusually punitive country. We now need to ask how well the experiment has worked.

Epidemic of Violence

The prison has become a looming presence in our society to an extent unparalleled in our history—or that of any other industrial democracy. Short of major wars, mass incarceration has been the most thoroughly implemented government social program of our time. And as with other government programs, it is reasonable to ask what we have gotten in return.

Let me be clear: there is legitimate dispute about the effects of imprisonment on crime, and people of goodwill can and do argue about the precise impact of the incarceration boom of the past twenty-five years. But the legitimate dispute takes place within very narrow boundaries, and the available evidence cannot be comforting to those who put great hopes on the prison experiment. Nor do we have reason to expect better results in the future; indeed, if anything, just the opposite.

Here, in a nutshell, is where we stand after more than two decades of the prison boom. The good news is that reported violent crime has declined in the country as a whole since about 1992—quite sharply in some cities—suggesting that, at least in most places, the worst of the epidemic of violence that rocked the country in the late 1980s and early 1990s has passed. But the bad news is extensive and troubling. First, most of the recent decline represents a leveling off from un-precedented *rises* in the preceding several years—and there-fore a longer time frame reveals no significant decline at all. Second, even that return to the norm has been disturbingly uneven, disproportionately accounted for by the experience of a few large cities, notably New York. Third, even in those cities violent crime often remains higher, and rarely more than fractionally lower, than it was before our massive in-vestment in incarceration began. Fourth, violence has *risen* dramatically over the past twenty-five years in many other cities, despite the prison boom and despite several other de-velopments that should have *reduced* violence. Fifth, the overall figures on trends in violent crime conceal a tragic ex-plosion of violence among the young and poor, which has yet to return to the already intolerably high levels of the mid-1980s. Finally, there is nothing in these patterns to re-assure us that an epidemic of violence won't erupt again. . . .

Half of America

The U.S. prison population has increased nearly 400% since 1980. A study by the Brookings Institution suggests that if our prison population continues to increase at the present rate, half of America will be in prison by the year 2053.

Alex Guerrero, *Harvard Crimson*, April 19, 2000.

Though the recent declines in violent crime have occurred in many cities across the country, moreover, a handful of cities account for a considerable proportion of the overall trend. There were about 137,000 fewer robberies in the United States in 1996 than in 1992; New York City alone contributed 41,000 of that total, or about 30 percent, and if we look back further in time, the picture appears consider-ably grimmer. An examination of homicide rates over the past quarter century in the hardest-hit American cities is a particularly sobering exercise. Again, there is some good news. Boston's homicide rate, for example, fell by about 3 percent between 1970 and 1995; San Francisco's, by about 13 percent. (New York—where the most notable recent declines in homicide have taken place—actually suffered an overall slight *rise* over this longer period, though it has fallen further since.) But there is also a great deal of *bad* news. Murder was up about 70 percent in Los Angeles, over 80 percent in Phoenix, over 90 percent in Oakland and Memphis. It more than doubled in Washington, Birmingham, Richmond, and Jackson, Mississippi. In Milwaukee and Rochester (N.Y.), homicide rates exploded by more than 200 percent in these years; in Minneapolis, by over 300 percent. In New Orleans, the homicide rate rose by a stunning 329 percent. . . .

Policies That Deprive

While we were busily jamming our prisons to the rafters with young, poor men, we were simultaneously generating the fastest rise in income inequality in recent history. We were tolerating the descent of several million Americans, most of them children, into poverty—a kind of poverty that, as study after study showed, became both deeper and more difficult to escape as time went on. An American child under eighteen was half again as likely to be poor in 1994 as twenty years earlier, and more and more poor children were spending a long stretch of their childhood, or all of it, below the poverty line. The poor, moreover, became increasingly isolated, spatially and economically, during these years— trapped in ever more impoverished and often chaotic neighborhoods, without the support of kin or friends, and surrounded by others in the same circumstances. At the same time, successive administrations cut many of the public supports—from income benefits to child protective services— that could have cushioned the impact of worsening economic deprivation and community fragmentation. And they also removed some of the rungs on our already wobbly ladders *out* of poverty: federal spending on jobs and job training for low-income people dropped by half during the 1980s. Meanwhile, between 1980 and 1993, federal spending on "correctional activities" rose, in current dollars, by 521 percent.

The results of these policies have been documented over and over again: communities without stable jobs, without preventive health care, without school guidance counselors or recreation facilities, with staggeringly inadequate mental health and child welfare services. . . .

The Default Solution

The prisons became, in a very real sense, a substitute for the more constructive social policies we were avoiding. A growing prison system was what we had *instead* of an antipoverty policy, instead of an employment policy, instead of a comprehensive drug-treatment or mental health policy. Or, to put it even more starkly, the prison *became* our employment policy, our drug policy, our mental health policy, in the vacuum left by the absence of more constructive efforts.

This is not just a metaphor. The role of the prison as a default "solution" to many American social problems is apparent when we juxtapose some common statistics that are rarely viewed in combination. We've seen, for example, that by the end of 1996 there were almost 1.7 million inmates—mostly poor and male—confined in American jails and prisons. Officially, those inmates are not counted as part of the country's labor force, and accordingly they are also not counted as unemployed. If they were, our official jobless rate would be much higher, and our much-vaunted record of controlling unemployment, as compared with other countries, would look considerably less impressive. Thus, in 1996 there was an average of about 3.9 million men officially unemployed in the United States, and about 1.1 million in state or federal prison. Adding the imprisoned to the officially unemployed would boost the male unemployment rate in that year by more than a fourth, from 5.4 to 6.9 percent. And that national average obscures the social implications of the huge increases in incarceration in some states. In Texas, there were about 120,000 men in prison in 1995, and 300,000 officially unemployed. Adding the imprisoned to the jobless count raises the state's male unemployment rate by well over a *third*, from 5.6 to 7.8 percent. If we conduct the same exercise for *black* men, the figures are even more thought-provoking. In 1995, there were 762,000 black men officially counted as unemployed, and another 511,000 in state or federal prison. Combining these numbers raises the jobless rate for black men by *two-thirds*, from just under 11 to almost 18 percent.

Consider also the growing role of the jails and prisons as a de facto alternative to a functioning system of mental health care. In California, an estimated 8 to 20 percent of state prison inmates and 7 to 15 percent of jail inmates are seriously mentally ill. Research shows, moreover, that the vast majority of the mentally ill who go behind bars are not being treated by the mental health system at the time of their arrest; for many, the criminal justice system is likely to be the first place they receive serious attention or even medication. The number of seriously mentally ill inmates in the jails and prisons may be twice that in state mental hospitals on any given day. In the San Diego County jail, 14 percent of male and 25 percent of female inmates were on psychiatric medication in the mid-1990s: The Los Angeles County jail system, where over 3,000 of the more than 20,000 inmates were receiving psychiatric services, is now said to be the largest mental institution in the United States—and also, according to some accounts, the largest homeless shelter.

Prison, then, has increasingly become America's social agency of first resort for coping with the deepening problems of a society in perennial crisis. And it is important to understand that, to some extent, the process has been self-perpetuating. Growing social disintegration has produced more violent crime; in turn, the fear of crime (often whipped up by careless and self-serving political rhetoric) has led the public and the legislatures to call for "tough" responses; the diversion of resources to the correctional system has aggravated the deterioration of troubled communities and narrowed the economic prospects for low-income people, who have maintained high levels of crime despite huge increases in incarceration; the persistence of violent crime paradoxically leads to calls for more of the same. And so the cycle continues.

"Even career criminals often give up crime because they don't want to go back to prison."

Imprisonment Reduces Crime

Morgan Reynolds

Imprisonment's role in reducing crime has met increased scrutiny since the U.S. prison population reached 2 million inmates in 1999. In the following viewpoint, Morgan Reynolds argues that imprisonment reduces crime by incapacitating career criminals and deterring others from committing offenses. The drop in the crime rate in the 1990s, Reynolds claims, was a result of the booming prison population. He maintains that America's high crime rates and high imprisonment rates do not reflect a flawed prison system, but the failure to imprison more offenders in previous years. Reynolds is an economics professor at Texas A&M University and the director of the Criminal Justice Center at the National Center for Policy Analysis.

As you read, consider the following questions:

1. According to Reynolds, which is a greater deterrent to crime, the certainty or severity of punishment?
2. How does Reynolds support his view that programs for juvenile offenders do not reduce crime as effectively as imprisonment?
3. In the author's opinion, what is the public's view of imprisonment?

Excerpted from Morgan Reynolds's testimony before the United States House of Representatives Committee on the Judiciary, Subcommittee on Crime, October 2, 2000, Washington, DC.

I appreciate the invitation to testify before the subcommittee today on the question of whether or not punishment works to reduce crime.

The answer is obvious to most Americans—yes, of course punishment reduces crime. Punishment converts criminal activity from a paying proposition to a nonpaying proposition, at least sometimes, and people respond accordingly.

We all are aware of how similar incentives work in our lives, for example, choosing whether or not to drive faster than the law allows. (How many of us in this room, for example, have run afoul of law enforcement on a traffic charge?) Incentives matter, including the risks we are willing to run. This is only a commonsense observation about how people choose to behave. Yet controversy over the very existence of a deterrence and incapacitation effect of incarceration has raged in elite circles.

Connecting the Dots

The first duty of a scientist, it's been said, is to point out the obvious. The logic of deterrence is pretty obvious, but I must point to evidence too, which is overwhelming, for the negative impact of punishment on crime. Evidence ranges from simple facts to sophisticated statistical and econometric studies.

Even experts who disagree with each other about some aspects of criminal justice are in agreement about deterrence. For example, when *Forbes* magazine asked John Lott, senior research scholar at Yale Law School and author of *More Guns Less Crime*, "Why the recent drop in crime?" he responded, "Lots of reasons—increases in arrest rates, conviction rates, prison sentence lengths." And Daniel Nagin, a Carnegie-Mellon University professor of public policy who co-authored an article in the *Journal of Legal Studies* critical of Lott's work on concealed carry laws, says in *The Handbook of Crime and Punishment*, Oxford, 1998, "The combined deterrent and incapacitation effect generated by the collective actions of the police, courts, and prison system is very large."

In sharp contrast to the situation ten years ago, experts who assert the contrary are fighting a rearguard action. Crime rates have fallen 30 percent over the last decade while the prison and jail population doubled to two million. Most people are able to connect these dots (the *New York Times* aside), and even the academy has caught on. As German philosopher Arthur Schopenhauer said, truth passes through three stages, first, it is ridiculed, second, it is violently opposed, and third, it is accepted as being self-evident. . . .

The Hard Reality

Given the avarice of man, the hard reality is that the threat of bad consequences, including public retribution posed by the legal system, is vital to secure human rights to life and property against predation. If men were angels, as James Madison said, we'd have no need of government.

The sad part about prisons is that the most effective crime reducer is the intact family. But government policies have gone far to undermine the family, intensifying the crime problem (welfare, taxes, no-fault divorce, etc.). As internal restraints (character, morality, virtue) degrade, we lamentably rely on external restraints to protect civilization, at least in the short run. As Edmund Burke, English political philosopher, said, "Society cannot exist unless a controlling power upon will and appetite be placed somewhere, and the less of it there is within, the more there must be without . . . men of intemperate minds cannot be free. Their passions forge their fetters."

Criminality is purposeful human behavior. The testimony of criminals provides perhaps our strongest evidence that, in the vast majority of cases, lawbreakers reason and act like other human beings (also a fundamental proposition in the justice system). Criminologists Richard Wright and Scott Decker interviewed 105 active, nonincarcerated residential burglars in St. Louis, Mo. Burglar No. 013 said, "After my eight years for robbery, I told myself then I'll never do another robbery because I was locked up with so many guys that was doin' 25 to 30 years for robbery and I think that's what made me stick to burglaries, because I had learned that a crime committed with a weapon will get you a lot of time.". . .

Which provides the greater deterrent, certainty or severity of punishment? One provocative study involving prisoners and college students came down firmly on the side of certainty. When tested, both groups responded in virtually identical terms. Prisoners could identify their financial self-interest in an experimental setting as well as students could. However, in their decision making, prisoners were much more sensitive to changes in certainty than in severity of punishment. In terms of real-world application, the authors of the study speculate that long prison terms are likely to be more impressive to lawmakers than lawbreakers.

Compare and Contrast

• During the 1980s, California increased its prison population at a rate faster than the nation and experienced a decline in serious crime relative to that of the nation.

• Texas, meanwhile, lagged in the growth of its prison population and its rate of serious crime shot up relative to that of the nation.

• The opposite has occurred during the 1990s, as Texas has enjoyed a 33 percent decline in serious crime while sharply increasing its prison population to the highest rate in the nation.

• By contrast, the growth in California's prison population has leveled off and now trails the national average, and California consequently is making only modest progress against serious crime.

National Center for Policy Analysis, September 24, 1998.

Supporting evidence for this viewpoint comes from a National Academy of Sciences panel which claimed that a 50 percent increase in the probability of incarceration prevents about twice as much violent crime as a 50 percent increase in the average term of incarceration.

Nonetheless, severity of punishment also remains crucial for deterrence. "A prompt and certain slap on the wrist," criminologist Ernest van den Haag wrote, "helps little." Or, as Milwaukee Judge Ralph Adam Fine wrote, "We keep our hands out of a flame because it hurt the very first time (not the second, fifth or 10th time) we touched the fire."

Crime Before and After Imprisonment

If the United States, with so many people in prison, has one of the world's highest crime rates, doesn't this imply that prison does not work? Scholar Charles Murray has examined this question and concluded that the answer is no. Instead, the nation has had to imprison more people in recent years because it failed to do so earlier (the war on drugs also plays a role).

Murray compared the record of the risk of imprisonment in England to that in the United States. In England the risk of going to prison for committing a crime fell by about 80 percent over a period of 40 years and the English crime rate gradually rose. By contrast, the risk of going to prison in the U.S. fell by 64 percent in just 10 years starting in 1961 and the U.S. crime rate shot up.

In the United States, it was not a matter of crimes increasing so fast that the rate of imprisonment could not keep up. Rather, the rate of imprisonment fell first by deliberate policy decisions. By the time the U.S. began incarcerating more criminals in the mid-1970s, huge increases were required to bring the risk of imprisonment up to the crime rate. It is more difficult to reestablish a high rate of imprisonment after the crime rate has escalated than to maintain a high risk of imprisonment from the outset, Murray concluded. We've experienced the same phenomenon in Texas, where crime rocketed up in the 1980s while punishment plunged.

However, both the U.S. and Texas experiences showed that it is possible for imprisonment to stop a rising crime rate and then gradually begin to push it down. The American crime rate peaked in 1980, a few years after the risk of imprisonment reached its nadir. Since then, as the risk of imprisonment has increased, with few exceptions the rates of serious crimes have retreated in fits and starts to levels of 20 or more years ago. My own research for the NCPA shows that expected punishment has had an inverse correlation with crime rates for both Texas and the nation.

Prevention vs. Detention

Juvenile offenders, due to their youth and immaturity, pose a special challenge to the criminal justice system. In the past, many judges and social workers have argued for less stringent treatment of such offenders, with "prevention" taking precedence over detention. The focus tends to be on so-called root causes, rehabilitation and nonpunitive approaches. Yet there is a close connection between lack of punishment and the forming of criminal habits. Recent studies note the effectiveness of punishment for juveniles, not just adults. Between 1980 and 1993 juvenile crime rose alarmingly, and as the states toughened their approach during the 1990s, it declined just as steeply.

Likewise, in his study of criminal justice in England, Charles Murray found that in 1954 the system operated on the assumption that the best way to keep crime down was to intervene early and sternly. Crime was very low, and the number of youths picked up by the police went down by about half as children matured from their early to their late teens. Today, however, a widespread assumption in England (as in the United States) is that youthful offenders need patience more than punishment. England's traditionally low crime rate is now very high, and the number of youths picked up by the police roughly triples from the early to the late teens.

The need to hold the individual juvenile criminal responsible for his actions does not make incarceration the sole option. For example, Anne L. Schneider found in six random-assignment experiments involving 876 adjudicated (convicted) delinquents in six American cities that victim restitution and incarceration both lowered re-offending while probation did not. Victim restitution meant monetary restitution, community service or work to repay the victims.

The Problematic Alternatives

Believers in rehabilitation regard punishment as primitive or counterproductive. For example, Alvin Bronstein, former executive director of the American Civil Liberties Union's National Prison Project, contended that releasing half the nation's prisoners would have little or no effect on the U.S. crime rate.

A major obstacle for such sunny optimism is the existence of what might be called the criminal personality. Perhaps the most important work on this subject is the three-volume study by the late Samuel Yochelson, a physician, and Stanton Samenow, a practicing psychologist. After interviewing hundreds of criminals and their relatives and acquaintances, the two researchers concluded that criminals have control over what they do, freely choosing evil over good, have distinct personalities, described in detail as deceitful, egotistical, myopic and violent and make specific errors in thinking (52 such errors are identified).

Yochelson and Samenow assert that the criminal must resolve to change and accept responsibility for his own behavior. Hardened criminals can reform themselves, but Samenow estimates that only 10 percent would choose to do so. He avoids the word "rehabilitation" when describing chronic criminals: "When you think of how these people react, how their patterns go back to age 3 or 4, there isn't anything to rehabilitate."

Careful studies of well-intended but soft-headed programs continue to find little payoff. In the case of street gang crime, Professor Malcolm Klein found that typical liberal-based gang interventions have failed to manifest much utility. They appeal to our best instincts, but are too indirect, too narrow or else produce boomerang effects by producing increased gang cohesiveness.

The truth is that changing criminal behavior by means other than deterrence is always problematical. A comprehensive scientific evaluation of hundreds of previous studies and prevention programs funded by the Justice Department found that "some programs work, some don't, and some may even increase crime." The report was prepared by the University of Maryland's Department of Criminology and Criminal Justice for the Justice Department and mandated by Congress. Still, too little is known and the report calls for 10 percent of all federal funding for these programs to be spent on independent evaluations of the impact of prevention programs.

Public opinion strongly supports the increased use of prisons to give criminals their just desserts. The endorsement of punishment is relatively uniform across social groups. More than three-quarters of the public see punishment as the primary justification for sentencing. More than 70 percent believe that incapacitation is the only sure way to prevent future crimes, and more than three-quarters believe that the courts are too easy on criminals. Three-quarters favor the death penalty for murder.

Still, the public holds out some hope for rehabilitation, too. About 60 percent express hope that services like psychological counseling, training and education inside prison will correct personal shortcomings. Such sentiments are more likely to be expressed on behalf of young offenders than adults, and by nonwhite respondents.

Unpleasant, Expensive, but Necessary

Despite continuing calls for a "better way," what criminals need most is evidence that their crimes do not pay. Neither criminals nor the rest of us "drive a car 100 miles an hour toward a brick wall, because we know what the consequences will be," as author Robert Bidinotto puts it. Punishment flat works. It's unpleasant and expensive, yes, but among other virtues, it supplies the convict with a major incentive to reform. Even career criminals often give up crime because they don't want to go back to prison. The old prescription that punishment be swift, certain and severe is affirmed by modern social science.

As expected punishment plunged during the 1960s and 1970s, crime rose astronomically. When expected punishment began rising in the 1980s and 1990s, crime leveled off and began falling. With the well-publicized success of no-nonsense police tactics like those in New York City, few observers today doubt that the criminal justice system can have a major impact on crime. Does that mean that everything has been done perfectly over the last decade? No, there is plenty of room for improvement in the future, but that is another subject.

"The common view of the prison is simplistic because it fails to account for the unintended consequences of imprisonment."

Imprisonment Does Not Reduce Crime

Todd R. Clear

In the following viewpoint, Todd R. Clear argues that to-day's high rate of imprisonment does not reduce crime. He insists that imprisonment is a flawed response to crime because it oversimplifies the crime problem. Clear argues that today's criminal justice system treats crime as a "phenomenon of individuals" and ignores the complex social and economic forces that shape criminal behavior. The transfer of large numbers of individuals from communities into prisons, he contends, may increase crime in those communities by removing the forces that inhibit criminal behavior, including family stability, neighborhood order, and economic well-being. Clear is a professor and associate dean of the School of Criminology and Criminal Justice at Florida State University at Tallahassee.

As you read, consider the following questions:
1. According to Clear, what is the "atomistic" view of crime?
2. What is the theory of vacancy-chains?
3. According to James Finkenhauer, why was the "Scared Straight" program unsuccessful?

Excerpted with permission from "Backfire: When Incarceration Increases Crime," by Todd R. Clear, 1996. Article available at www.doc.state.ok.us/DOCS/OCJRC/Ocjrc96/Ocjrc7.htm.

In the popular point of view, prisons are thought of as crime fighting-devices: exposing offenders to prison reduces crime. This viewpoint began governing penal policy in the early 1970s; since then, we have increased the size of our prison population fivefold.

However, the expansion of the penal system has not been accompanied by an equivalent decrease in crime. The failure of this extraordinary increase in incarceration to produce a meaningful reduction in crime needs explanation. . . . The common view of the prison is simplistic because it fails to account for the unintended consequences of imprisonment. These unforeseen effects are subtle and, in some ways, modest, but over time they combine to counteract the positive effects of prison. A broader, more complete understanding of the effects of incarceration would enable us to understand the limits of using prison as a crime-prevention strategy.

The debate about incarceration policy has been dominated by an atomistic view of crime—that individuals who engage in crime are influenced by personal motivations, independent of the contexts in which they live. The sole exception to this view is that the threat of incarceration prevents people from carrying out their illicit desires. Consequently, decisions to engage in crime are seen as products of the likelihood and degree of punishment if caught, and little else.

An alternative view of criminal behavior employs a more holistic perception of the potential offender—as a person who lives in places, interacts with fellow citizens, and responds to various life circumstances with choices based on a grounded understanding of the consequences of those choices. The use of prison might affect all of these contextual elements: the places people live, the social interactions occurring there, the choices people have available to them, and their understanding of those choices.

Crime as a Phenomenon of Individuals

Throughout this century, conversation about crime policy has been dominated by the idea that individual offenders require reform or rehabilitation. The belief now in vogue is that they require control. Of course, these approaches differ in several important respects, but they share a common analytic foundation: Crime and its control are best understood in regard to the thoughts and emotions of specific individuals who commit crimes or want to commit crimes.

These views might all be termed "atomistic" because offenders are seen as individual actors who behave largely in isolation from their environments. Therefore, rehabilitation models have always treated the offender as the unit of analysis, to be diagnosed or classified for correctional interventions based on his or her individual characteristics. . . . The tendency to view crime as a phenomenon defined by wayward individuals and their desires is not only ingrained in penology, it is reinforced in public consciousness by the popular media's focus on individual criminal events as news stories.

The dominant viewpoint is atomistic in another sense: Incarcerating specific offenders is considered to be a self-contained process—affecting that offender and almost nobody else. The walls of the prison stand symbolically as a black box into which citizens disappear for a time and later emerge, changed or not. The number of black boxes in existence and the frequency of experiences within them are, therefore, important only for the individuals who go through the process. This perspective ignores the potential impact of incarceration upon families, communities, economics, and politics. . . .

The Replacements

We already lock up a million offenders. Do we have all the wrong ones? Since 1973, we have increased the prison population by 800,000 offenders. When we remove active offenders from society, crime rates do not drop nearly as much as we would expect. This suggests that street criminals are being replaced, that increases in imprisonment lead to increases in crime, or some combination of the two.

Albert Reiss was the first scholar to consider how replacement of criminals may affect crime rates during periods of high incarceration. He coined the term co-offending to refer to the fact that a large percentage of crime is committed by offenders behaving in groups. This is particularly characteristic of drug crimes and violent street crimes, such as robbery. The question is the degree to which the apprehension and incarceration of one member of a co-offending group ends the criminality of the group or merely causes the group to recruit a new member. A related question is the degree to which the recruitment process enlists persons who otherwise would not have been involved in the criminal behavior.

[Criminologists S. Ekland-Olson, W.R. Kelley, H-J Loo, J. Olbrich and M. Eisenberg] have used the term vacancy-chains to refer to the process by which replacement may cancel out the crime-prevention benefits of incapacitation. This is particularly pertinent to drug markets. The incarceration of drug offenders, in the face of a stable demand for drugs, creates job openings in the drug delivery enterprise and allows for an ever-broadening recruitment of citizens into the illegal trade. This has led to speculation that policing and incarcerating drug offenders results in greater involvement of younger males as workers in the drug market. Replacement theories are especially applicable to street gangs. When one or two gang members is arrested, the criminality of the remaining gang members is unaffected. Gang researchers find that up to a certain threshold, arrests do not have much impact on gang criminality. . . .

The Diminished Power of Deterrence

In theory, prison suppresses crime because prison is an authentically unpleasant and stigmatizing experience that people seek to avoid. These effects are dependent on images of prison—how people understand the prison experience personally and socially. People think of imprisonment and imagine what it would be like to be there, what it would mean to have a record. These images inform the person's view of the pain and stigma that would result from being imprisoned. . . .

It is certainly the case that public debate projects a changed view of prison's unpleasantness. A national movement to strip prisons of television sets and weight lifting privileges is motivated by what appears to be a conviction that prisons are simply not tough enough. The belief that prison time is easy compared to life on the streets is widely shared. It has been voiced by politicians such as Governor William Weld and Senator Phil Gramm, researcher Joan Petersilia, and even civil rights advocate Jesse Jackson. While each commentator would suggest a different course of action in response to this observation, it is interesting nonetheless that they agree our prisons are "not so bad."

This is an important issue because, if people's images of the prison are less severe, then the associated desire to avoid the experience can be expected to diminish. Where did the remarkable idea that our prisons are places of comfort originate?

A Terrible Cycle

[Dina R.] Rose, a sociologist in New York's John Jay College of Criminal Justice, found that in high-crime Tallahassee [Florida] neighborhoods that were otherwise comparable, crime reductions were lower in those with the greatest number of people moving in and out of prison. With high incarceration rates, she argues, prison can be transformed from a crime deterrent into a factor that fuels a cycle of crime and disorder by breaking up families, souring attitudes toward the criminal justice system and leaving communities populated with too many people hardened by the experience of going to prison.

Michael A. Fletcher, *Washington Post*, July 19, 1999.

There are several sources. Two decades of prisoner rights litigation created a public belief that prisoners can effectively resist arbitrary or brutal treatment. New prisons do not resemble menacing, dungeon-like structures with unscaleable walls; instead, they are attractive brick edifices surrounded by fences. Popular media portrayals of prison life may also contribute to a growing public conviction that prisons are not harsh.

But there is another possibility: The increased use of prison over the last 20 years may have reduced the negative view of prison. The more often the sanction of imprisonment is employed, the less it deters.

It is plausible that deterrence is linked to mystery. People imagine a harsh and forbidding environment in which brutal and victimizing experience is commonplace. They also imagine the shame and humiliation that follows others learning of their prison history. These are vivid images, but the reality of prison experience, more widely distributed among the populace, may soften this mental portrait.

James Finkenauer's study of Rahway Prison's "Scared Straight" program illustrates this idea. The program involved sending first-time juvenile offenders to meet with a group of lifers, who would regale them with terrifying stories about prison and threatening behavior about "what I am gonna do to you if you end up here." The theory behind the program was that these juveniles, dabbling in delinquency, would be so frightened by the crusty lifers' tales that they would be "scared straight"— frightened into obedience with the law in order to avert the inevitably horrifying prison experience.

Finckenauer found that the kids who went through the program actually did worse than a comparison group not exposed to the program. The kids in his study were exposed to the most hostile version of prison life imaginable, and yet far from being scared straight, they were likely to keep offending. Several explanations of this finding are possible, but the most obvious is that exposure to the brutalizing nature of prison normalizes the experience and provides images of survival to replace pre-existing images of doom. The youth now have a grounded experience of prison at its most brutal, and of tough men not only surviving the experience but thriving within it. Finally, that the youth themselves survived their prison experience diminishes the mystery of prison life. Popular American images of the prison were dominated by the "big house" myth and Edward G. Robinson [American film actor] tough-guy characters. Real-life experience replaces popular ideation with grounded reality. . . .

The more prison is used, the more real are the images people have of prison. As these images are normalized, their mythological potency is diminished and so is the prison's power to deter criminal behavior.

Some who have commented that today's prison life is "not so bad" have in turn argued for making the conditions more brutal. If my analysis is correct, they are fighting a losing battle. It is not the actual brutality of prison life that deters, it is imagining the prison experience. No matter how brutal—and today's prisons can be undeniably cruel places—the widespread use of prison will continue to create growing numbers of informed consumers who know people who have survived and count them among friends and family.

Indirect Ways in Which Imprisonment May Increase Crime

We can question whether the expanded use of incarceration may exacerbate the social conditions of crime, thus contributing indirectly to increases in crime. Broadly, three sets of social forces may be negatively affected by prison: families and children, neighborhood order, and social inequality. . . .

Families and children. The effects of incarceration on children and families are emotional and material. Material effects include problems that result from the loss of child care and financial support. In the process of responding to the disruption, secondary changes may also occur such as address or school changes, changes in the composition of the family unit, and reductions in financial security.

The emotional consequences are less obvious but potentially more significant. Depending on the age of the child, removal of a parent to prison may promote acting out, especially in school. Children may feel shame, humiliation, and a loss of social status. They may come to distrust or even despise the symbols of authority (laws and the state) that have removed their parent. The chances of new parenting combinations increase, and this may mean more inconsistent or fractious relationships and disciplinary practices with children.

Some might argue that removing a criminal parent likely removes an abusive or abusing influence from the home. The net gain of removing such a parent may outweigh the net loss, but it may not. Nevertheless, a child will respond in a variety of ways, some of which are negative. Specifically, the future criminality by children of incarcerated parents is worth exploring. Certainly, poor school performance, unsupervised free time, financial strain, decreased contact with adults, and suppressed anger are precursors of delinquency. . . .

Neighborhood order. Incarceration removes persons who could provide surveillance value in neighborhoods. And, fewer adults means less social interaction. The entry and exit of adults from families means that the economic circumstances of those families change—this in turn promotes relocation, which creates transitory populations and often less integrated neighborhoods.

The neighborhoods from which people (especially young

men) are removed to prison are the places they return upon their release from prison. These ex-offenders are more likely to be unemployed or underemployed, adding to the local unemployment rate and the chronic difficulties ex-convicts face in finding and retaining work. In short, the more the prison system grows, the more it contributes to the decay of neighborhoods outside its walls—inner-city locations already struggling with the strains of economic and social disorder. . . .

Economic inequality. The role of inequality in crime is well-established, as is its role in punishment. Expanding the prison system aggravates socioeconomic inequalities in two main ways: imprisonment narrows the life-chances of persons exposed to it and indirectly results in shifts of economic resources from urban settings to other locations.

It is well-known that imprisonment damages employment possibilities, though the degree of damage is disputed. . . . These effects of incarceration are probably small compared to the economic relocation of resources. Each prisoner represents an economic asset that has been removed from that community and placed elsewhere. As an economic being, the person would spend money at or near his or her area of residence— typically, an inner city. Imprisonment displaces that economic activity: Instead of buying cigarettes and snacks in a local deli, the prisoner makes those purchases in a prison commissary.

The removal of the prisoner may represent a moderate loss of economic value to the home community, but it is a boon to the prison community. Each prisoner represents as much as $25,000 in income for the community in which the prison is located, not to mention the value of constructing the prison facility in the first place. This can be a massive transfer of value; a young male worth a few thousand dollars of support to children and local purchases is transformed into a $25,000 financial asset to a rural prison community. The economy of the rural community is artificially amplified, while the local city economy is artificially deflated.

Of course, there are other ways that the prison may increase relative disadvantage. Financial loss suffered by children and partners of the imprisoned, long-term damage caused by interruptions in the normal life cycles of these families, and effects on the social status of ex-convicts also contribute to a legacy of economic inequality. The fact that prison experiences are concentrated in a handful of neighborhoods targets those places as especially harmed by the expanded use of incarceration. Thus, it is not surprising to discover that the place a person goes to when released from prison is a good predictor of the likelihood that the person will remain arrest free.

"*If having a privatized prison system means prisoners will actually serve the time they deserve, then a private prison system is ideal.*"

Privatization Would Benefit the Prison System

Jeff Becker

Overcrowding has become a major challenge of U.S. prisons, threatening the security of prisons and the safety of the public. Jeff Becker argues, in the following viewpoint, that allowing private companies to build and maintain prisons can help ease the burden of overcrowding endured by federal and state facilities. He claims that private prisons are run as safely as public prisons. Private prisons can also preserve public safety, he contends, because increased prison space means more inmates will carry out longer sentences. Becker is an undergraduate at Texas A&M University and contributor to the *Battalion*, Texas A&M's student newspaper

As you read, consider the following questions:

1. According to Becker, why is it not a conflict of interest to make a profit from prisons?
2. In Becker's view, for what aspects of operations should private prisons be liable for?
3. What are the author's opinions of rehabilitation and early release programs?

Excerpted from "Benefits of Prison Privatization Outweigh Alleged Disadvantages," by Jeff Becker, *The Batallion*, June 22, 1999. Reprinted with permission from *The Batallion*.

P rivate prisons are a growing sector of the U.S. economy. With incarceration rates on the rise in this country, corporations such as the Correction Corporation of America (CCA) stand to profit from all the criminals being put behind bars. These companies are state-contracted, and they privately own and operate some of the facilities housing America's felons.

Many question the government's decision to dole out its authority and responsibility to house those guilty of serious crimes to private companies trying to make a profit.

This question is especially relevant to Texans, because Texas houses the most criminals in private prisons of all the states, at around 30,000.

The benefits of *prison* privatization far outweigh any of its supposed disadvantages.

Opponents claim private prisons do not have the same level of security that public prisons have and that prisoners are more likely to escape, citing an incident at a CCA-run prison where six inmates were able to cut a hole in a fence and escape.

Caring About Profits—and Security

Security is always going to be the biggest issue at any prison, public or private.

However, there are going to be occasional security breaches, as Texas residents found out with the recent escape of an inmate from the high-security Huntsville prison, which is a public prison.

One cannot base a reputation on one incident.

Just because there was an escape at a prison does not mean the people there do not care about security.

Private prisons want to make a profit, and it would be very self-destructive for them not to care about security, because if they did not they obviously would not be allowed to operate for long.

Caring about both profits and security does not create a conflict of interest.

In a recent *Washington Post* article, U.S. Representative Ted Strickland stated private prisons have "potentially corrupting effects on public policy."

He further said prison corporations like the CCA could become powerful lobbyists in Congress for long-term and mandatory sentencing in order to maximize profits.

But this complaint is unfounded. Most people would like nothing more than to see violent criminals go to jail for longer periods of time. In the last two decades, the incarceration rate in the United States has tripled, and the violent crime rate has fallen. Most people would like this trend to continue.

Strickland also suggests that since private prisons control good conduct reports, they may have the tendency to give bad reports in order to keep the prisoners in jail as long as possible, again, to maximize profits. Someone who is in for a 50-year sentence may actually serve the full time.

Stating that prisoners may actually go full-term in private prisons cannot possibly be used as an argument against their existence.

One of the biggest complaints about the prison system today is that people are getting out early who should not be out on the streets.

If having a privatized prison system means prisoners will actually serve the time they deserve, then a private prison system is ideal.

Addressing Liability

Another question surrounding private prisons is liability. Prisoners sue the state on account of the prison system all the time, and the question of who is responsible has to be asked.

If a private prison is charged with [a violation], who would be liable, the state or the prison corporation?

The state gives the authority to the private prisons to hold prisoners, and it is responsible for the people who it deems not worthy for living in normal society.

This is important, because the state should not be handing out the authority to house felons to just anyone.

However, if the state is completely responsible for prisoners, this leaves no responsibility for the owners of the prisons, which would be bad for the state.

Private prisons must be liable for many of the aspects of operation in a prison, such as fair treatment and proper staff-to-inmate ratios. The state must be able to use the valuable

Advantages and Innovations

Private prisons enjoy several advantages over publicly operated prisons with regard to costs and operational expenditures. Privately built prisons are "likely to use innovative new design techniques, with sight lines and technology that allow inmates to be monitored with fewer correctional personnel," a RPPI [Reason Public Policy Institute] report said. Privately run prisons also employ fewer administrative levels. According to a private prison administrator, private prisons use about one-third the administrative personnel government prisons use.

Reason Public Policy Institute, *Spectrum*, Summer 1998.

tool of oversight in the implementation and operation of private prisons, in order to prevent being charged with violations that the prison corporation should be responsible for.

Easing the Prison System's Load

The main argument in favor of private prisons centers around money. The corrections corporations bid on prospects for the facilities, and the state government has the final say on when, where, and by whom these are built. Obviously, the corporation with the lowest bid would win.

This can be much cheaper than building a public prison. If a single prison can be built for less, then more prisons can be built for the same amount of money.

Also, in most private prisons the cost per prisoner is lower, which creates lower maintenance costs.

Overcrowding is the single biggest problem in the prison industry today. Over the past 30 years, prisoners' rights groups have brought numerous suits concerning unconstitutional conditions in prisons.

In 12 states, the entire state prison system either is or has been under court order concerning overcrowding.

To solve overcrowding, private prisons are a better alternative to early release programs.

A large percentage of the crime committed in this country is perpetrated by people who have already served hard time. The doctrine of rehabilitation for the most part has failed, and another alternative to the overcrowding problem must be evaluated. Potentially dangerous criminals cannot be dumped back on the street.

Private prisons are a good way to save taxpayers money and will help keep dangerous people away from the public.

In a time when the U.S. prison population exceeds 1 million people, the bottom line must be considered. Private prisons will help to ease overcrowding, help keep violent offenders off the streets for longer, and they will be able to do it for less money.

The benefits are obvious, and the corrections industry should be allowed to grow and ease the public prison system's back-breaking load.

> *"Research indicates that governments save little or no money by contracting out their prison business."*

Privatization Would Not Benefit the Prison System

Barry Yeoman

In the following viewpoint, Barry Yeoman argues that the prison system would not benefit from privatization. Private prisons do not save taxpayers money, he claims, but generate significant revenues for the private companies that run them. Yeoman insists that private prisons cut programs to increase profit, despite putting the safety of prisoners, staff, and communities in jeopardy. Yeoman is the senior staff writer at the *Independent*, an alternative newspaper based in Durham, North Carolina.

As you read, consider the following questions:
1. In Yeoman's opinion, why has the private prison industry grown so dramatically?
2. What examples does the author give to support his claim that private prisons across the nation are troubled?
3. According to Yeoman, how did inmates escape the Youngstown, Ohio, private prison?

Excerpted from "Steel Town Lockdown," by Barry Yeoman, *Mother Jones*, May/June 2000. Copyright © 2000 by Foundation for National Progress. Reprinted with permission from *Mother Jones*.

Not since slavery has an entire American industry derived its profits exclusively from depriving human beings of their freedom—not, at least, until a handful of corporations and Wall Street investors realized they could make millions from what some critics call "dungeons for dollars." Since the 1980s, when privatization became the rage for many government services, companies like CCA [Corrections Corporation of America] and its rival, Wackenhut Corporation, have been luring elected officials with a worry-free solution to prison overcrowding. Claiming they can lock people up cheaper than government can, the companies build cells on speculation, then peddle the beds to whatever local or state government needs a quick fix for its growing criminal population. "It's a heady cocktail for politicians who are trying to show they're tough on crime and fiscally conservative at the same time," says Judith Greene, a senior justice fellow at the Open Society Institute, a foundation chaired by philanthropist George Soros.

Over the past decade, private prisons have boomed. Corporations now control 122,900 beds for U.S. inmates, up at least eightfold since 1990. The reason is simple: With anti-drug laws and stiffer mandatory sentences pushing the prison population above two million, and governments strapped for capital to build new cells, for-profit prisons seem to offer plenty of cells at below-market prices. "If it could not be done cheaper than the government does it, then we wouldn't be in business now," says Brian Gardner, warden of the CCA prison in Youngstown, Ohio. "We believe in giving the taxpayer the best deal."

In fact, research indicates that governments save little or no money by contracting out their prison business. In 1996, the U.S. General Accounting Office reviewed five studies of private prisons and found no "substantial evidence" that for-profit institutions save taxpayer dollars. A more recent report commissioned by the U.S. attorney general notes that private prisons attempt to save money by cutting back on staffing, security, and medical care.

No company has benefited more from this private-prison boom—or been so plagued by understaffing, high turnover, and lax security—than CCA. The company, which controls half of a billion-dollar industry, now operates the sixth-largest prison system in the country—trailing only California, Texas, the U.S. Bureau of Prisons, New York, and Florida. Founded in 1983, CCA has never wanted for business. It now manages 82 prisons with 73,000 beds in 26 states, Puerto Rico, Great Britain, and Australia—raking in $365 million during the first three quarters of 1999.

Yet from the very beginning—when inmates from Texas escaped through the air-conditioner slots of a motel the company used as a makeshift penitentiary—CCA has engaged in cost cutting that jeopardizes the safety of prisoners, guards, and communities. In two Georgia prisons, the company's neglect of medical care and security amounted to "borderline deliberate indifference," according to a 1999 state audit. In Colorado [in 1999], a number of female guards left alone with hundreds of male inmates admitted having sex with prisoners in exchange for protection. And at a South Carolina juvenile facility, children were hog-tied and beaten by an overworked, undertrained staff, according to a lawsuit filed in federal court. "They were grabbing the kids and slamming their heads into walls, slamming them into the floors," says Gaston Fairey, an attorney representing one of the children.

What's more, escapes from CCA prisons have been rampant. According to one survey, at least 79 inmates fled CCA facilities nationwide between 1995 and 1998—compared to nine escapes from California prisons, which have more than twice as many inmates. Many of the breakouts could have been prevented, a report prepared for Attorney General Janet Reno concluded, if CCA had simply learned from its previous mistakes and "implemented preventive measures.". . .

For Good Measure?

By the mid-'90s, with unemployment still in the double digits, Youngstown was desperate for any job it could land. So when the world's largest private-prison company offered to employ 350 people, local officials welcomed it with tax breaks and free water and sewer hookups. As the new prison went up on the edge of town, it looked much like an old steel mill, only surrounded by razor wire. And it held the same promise for the men and women who applied for the $24,600-a-year jobs CCA offered.

But it didn't take long for disillusionment to set in. The day Victoria Wheeler reported for work as a guard, she recalls, the company "explained that these were going to be very, very bad inmates." CCA was negotiating a $182 million contract with the District of Columbia, which was scrambling to transfer some of its most unmanageable inmates out of a crumbling prison complex in Lorton, Virginia. Margaret Moore, director of the D.C. Department of Corrections, told the local newspaper that Youngstown's newest male residents would be "young, aggressive, and violent."

The Prison-Industrial Complex

The prison-industrial complex perpetuates itself. It is those who make the laws to put more and more people in jail who have the most to lose if the system slows down. Politicians, who receive millions in campaign contributions from companies making millions off the prison-industrial complex, create the laws that are becoming less and less lenient.

Andrew Hartman, *Humanist*, November/December 2000.

The first inmates arrived on May 15, 1997—courtesy of a transport company owned by CCA. Many of them were classified as maximum security, in violation of CCA's agreement with the city. Half came without case histories or medical records. And according to the report prepared for the U.S. attorney general's office, they arrived in such large numbers that they completely overwhelmed the prison. Inmates needed bedding and toiletries; they needed health screenings; their property needed to be inventoried and distributed. The prison's skeletal crew couldn't possibly accommodate so many new arrivals—900 in the first 17 days—especially after they discovered that many of the men's possessions hadn't arrived from D.C. "It was chaos," Wheeler says.

Angry and frustrated, some new arrivals refused to return to their cells one day until they received their personal property. When inmates in one unit threatened to "trash the place," prison officials ordered a full-scale teargassing of four cell blocks through a hatch on the roof. The gas, intended for outdoor use, blackened the blocks where it was dropped. "The entire pod was smoked out. You couldn't see through the gas," recalls Anthony Beshara, a former guard. Even after the men returned to their bunks and the prison's security chief gave an "all-clear" signal, court records show, the assault continued. "Three for good measure!" an assistant warden announced as the canisters fell. . . .

If CCA intended the show of force to make the prison more secure, it didn't work. That summer, six inmates escaped on a bright afternoon and one remained at large for several weeks. According to a report by the D.C. Corrections Trustee responsible for monitoring the private prison, everything that could have gone wrong did. A metal detector broke, a motion detector malfunctioned, and the outside yard went unsupervised for 40 minutes. (One staff member was inside playing Ping-Pong.) At the time of the break, there were 219 prisoners in the yard. "Fortunately," the trustee reported, "large numbers of inmates did not choose to . . . follow the route of these six."

Youngstown residents were alarmed by the escapes, but even those most experienced in community organizing didn't know how to take on a far-flung corporation like CCA. "Once the private prison opened, there didn't seem to be a heck of a lot that one could do to tear it down," says Staughton Lynd, an educator and labor lawyer with four decades of experience as an activist, dating back to his stint as director of the Mississippi Freedom Schools. Some residents put their energy into developing a visitation program to help prisoners' families make the 600-mile round trip from Washington. Senator [Bob] Hagan pushed a bill through the legislature putting tighter restrictions on for-profit prisons. . . .

Bad Publicity Brings Reform

In May 1999, inmates at the Youngstown prison won $1.65 million in a class-action lawsuit settlement with the company. Under the terms of the agreement, CCA agreed to pay damages to prisoners, improve security and medical care without cutting back other programs, and pay for an independent monitor to check company abuses. The settlement solves "the worst of the abuse," says Alphonse Gerhardstein, the inmates' attorney. The maximum-security prisoners have been shipped out. Sworn enemies are kept apart. The company has built three new guard towers and put up additional fences. And the prison sponsored more than 50,000 hours of staff training [in 1999], in areas such as conflict resolution and escape prevention.

The Youngstown facility currently appears to enjoy the institutional calm of a well-behaved high school, with murals on the cinderblock walls, monitors in every hallway, and well-stocked classrooms where inmates learn wiring, masonry, and commercial cleaning. And the prison's current leadership tries to distance itself from the earlier debacles. "The past is the past," says assistant chief Jason Medlin. "That was a different administration, a different system altogether."

But Gerhardstein warns that the improved conditions shouldn't be taken as proof that the company—much less the industry—has reformed. After all, he says, it took a lawsuit, new legislation, a renegotiated contract with the city, a monitoring program, and a whole lot of bad publicity just to get CCA to improve conditions at one facility.

For now, negotiations over the proposed expansion have been stalled by CCA's current financial upheaval. Last year, the company merged with a real-estate trust it set up called Prison Realty that was exempt from $50 million in federal income taxes. . . .

Unethical and Counterproductive

Paul Marcone, chief of staff to [Ohio State Representative James] Traficant, insists that negotiations for the proposed expansion in Youngstown will reopen soon. "CCA has had some organizational shake-ups," he says, "but now the company is focused more on expanding."

That expansion, many residents fear, would make Youngstown as synonymous with prisons as it was with steel a quarter-century ago. "We may have concentrated the sun's rays somewhat, but it's not clear if we've started a fire," says Lynd, whose Prison Forum is launching a campaign called Schools, Not Jails. Lynd and other opponents want to keep the debate above the level of "not in my backyard"—to convince the public and policymakers that it's both unethical and counterproductive to turn incarceration over to the private sector.

"We can't put somebody in the Black Hole of Calcutta, or the Gulag Archipelago, just because they've done something wrong," says Bob Hagan. "When money's your main motivation, you forget one major lesson: that these people are coming out. If you don't create rehabilitated prisoners, but you only create profit for your shareholders, then you have failed at a system that's supposed to protect society."

Periodical Bibliography

The following articles have been selected to supplement the diverse views presented in this chapter. Addresses are provided for periodicals not indexed in the *Readers' Guide to Periodical Literature*, the *Alternative Press Index*, the *Social Sciences Index*, or the *Index to Legal Periodicals and Books*.

Dan Baum	"Invisible Nation," *Rolling Stone*, December 7, 2000.
Pam Belluck	"As More Prisons Go Private, States Seek Tighter Controls," *The New York Times*, April 15, 1999.
Ellis Cose	"The Prison Paradox," *Newsweek*, November 13, 2000.
Norm Dean and Jeff Goodale	"Jails for the New Millennium: Choose the Right Technology, Build for Expansion," *American Jails*, January/February 2000. Available from American Jail Association, 2053 Day Rd., Suite 100, Hagerstown, MD 21740-9795.
Douglas Dennis	"Money Talks," *Angolite*, January/February 1997. Available from Louisiana State Penitentiary, Angola, LA 70712.
John J. DiIulio Jr.	"No Angels Fill Those Cells," *Law Enforcement Alliance of America (LEAA) Advocate*, Winter 1997. Available from the Law Enforcement Alliance of America, 7700 Leesburg Pike, Suite 421, Falls Church, VA 22043.
Jennifer Gonnerman	"Two Million and Counting," *Village Voice*, February 22, 2000. Available from 36 Cooper Square, New York, NY 10003.
Sam Hine	"The Prison Boom: Corporate Profits, Human Losses," *Witness*, November 1998.
Robert E. Moffit and David B. Mulhausen	"America's Prisons Are Full—of Criminals," *Human Events*, June 21, 2000. Available from One Massachusetts Ave. NW, Washington, DC 20001.
William Raspberry	"A Quarter of the World's Prison Inmates," *Liberal Opinion Week*, January 11, 1999. Available from PO Box 880, Vinton, IA 52349.
Jeanie M. Thies	"Prisons and Host Communities: Debunking the Myths and Building Community Relations," *Corrections Today*, April 2000. Available from the American Correctional Association, 4380 Forbes Blvd., Lanham, MD 20706-4322.
Anamaria Wilson	"Lock 'Em Up!" *Time*, February 14, 2000.

How Should Prisons Treat Inmates?

Chapter Preface

J.B. Stevens entered the Missouri prison system at age seventeen. He weighed 135 pounds, was saddled with drug problems, and faced a thirty-seven year sentence. In prison, he began weight training. By the time he was twenty-five, he tipped the scales at an athletic 175 pounds, had acquired his GED, and had hope for the future despite the many years in prison ahead of him. In explaining his rehabilitation, Stevens said, "The very first goals I set for myself in bodybuilding are today the cornerstones of my self-confidence. Everything I have achieved and everything I shall ever aspire to is owed to that simple beginning—weight training."

Supporters of weight training in prison contend that the benefits go beyond the rehabilitation of inmates. They insist that it keeps prisons safer because it provides a nonviolent means for inmates to relieve pent-up stress. In addition, weight training privileges can be used as an incentive for inmates to behave.

However, opponents to weight training in prison argue that it is an expensive leisure activity that should not be paid for by taxpayers. They claim many inmates sustain injuries from weight training, and the costs of these injuries make up a significant portion of prisons' medical bills. In 1994, the Arizona Department of Corrections removed weightlifting equipment from their prisons when orthopedic treatment bills exceeded $600,000 in a six-month period. Most of all, critics warn that weight training programs are bulking up inmates, potentially making them stronger criminals. One woman's testimony summarizes this fear, "I consider myself exceptionally strong for a woman. However, that strength didn't help me when a prison-reformed, weightlifting-enhanced convict on parole raped me."

Weight training is one of the many issues surrounding the debate of the treatment of inmates. The viewpoints in the following chapter examine the many programs and techniques used to treat inmates, which reflect differing opinions on the purpose of imprisonment.

> *"The idea of just punishment . . . recaptures the lost community of moral and legal elements which once characterized crime and punishment."*

Prisons Should Punish Inmates

Francis T. Murphy

In the following viewpoint, Francis T. Murphy claims that efforts to rehabilitate criminals are ineffective. Murphy contends that rehabilitating criminals in minimally safe, unstable, and inhumane institutions such as prisons is not likely. He concludes that a return to swift, certain punishment in prisons can restore the effectiveness of the criminal justice system in enforcing morality and deterring crime. Murphy is the presiding justice of the New York Supreme Court Appellate Division First Judicial Department.

As you read, consider the following questions:
1. According to the author, how did the idea of prisons originate?
2. In Murphy's view, what therapeutic interventions have characterized the "rehabilitative ideal"?
3. What two directions of penal policy does Murphy oppose?

Reprinted from "Moral Accountability and the Rehabilitative Ideal," by Francis T. Murphy, *New York State Bar Journal*, January 1984. Reprinted with permission from the New York State Bar Association *Journal*, January 1984, vol. 56, no. 1, published by the New York State Bar Association, 1 Elk St., Albany, NY 12207.

When a man is sentenced and led from courtroom to prison, two statements have been made as the door closes behind him. The judge has spoken to his crime, and society has spoken of how it will deal with him. Embedded in these statements is a fascinating complex of ideas about the nature of man, morality, law, and politics.

Prior to the 1800's, the prison system was unknown. Society's answer to the felon was usually given at the end of a rope or the swing of an axe. In imposing sentence, a judge was virtually a clerk, for he had no discretion in the matter. He simply sent the defendant to a death commanded by law.

During the first half of the 1800's, however, a confluence of ideas and political events produced the prison in America. So unusual was the idea of the prison that Europeans came to America in order to visit prisons and record what they saw.

A Humane Answer

How did the idea of the prison originate? In part, the prison was a humane answer to the criminal. Hanging a man for stealing a spoon or forging a note seemed immoral. In great part, the prison was an economic indulgence, for prior to the Industrial Revolution society could not have afforded prisons. Yet, lying behind humane motives and the new economy was a belief that included much more than the prison. The first half of the 1800's was an age of reform. Belief in the perfectibility of human beings and in the improvement of their social institutions was prevalent. In America and Europe a liberalism traceable to thinkers like John Locke and Desiderius Erasmus, to the Renaissance and ancient Greece, had as its central principle that to every question there was a rational answer, that man was able to discover rational solutions to his problems, and when thus enlightened he could live in a harmonious society. It was natural that a belief of that magnitude, infused into economic and social problems of every kind, and joined with a humanitarian spirit and the new, industrial wealth, would inhibit the tying of the rope and the swinging of the axe. Thus it was that the first half of the 1800's introduced in America not only the prison as a place for punishment and deterrence, but the prison as a place for the rehabilitative ideal, today condemned by many as the right idea in the wrong place.

The Rehabilitative Ideal

A usable definition of the rehabilitative ideal is that a primary purpose of penal treatment is the changing of the character and behavior of the prisoner in order to protect society and to help him. It is an idea that has attracted groups who march to the beat of very different drums. It has attracted those who think of crime as an individual's moral failure, or as an evil caused by corrupt social institutions, or as an entry in the printout of a prisoner's genetic program. Accordingly, the rehabilitative ideal has elicited different means—extending from the early 1800's imposition of absolute silence upon all prisoners in New York, and the unrelieved solitary confinement of all prisoners in Pennsylvania, to the twentieth century's faith in therapeutic interventions, such as the promoting of literacy, the teaching of vocational skills, the use of psychotherapy, and the less popular surgical removal of brain tissue. All of these means have one thing in common. Each has failed as a reliable rehabilitative technique and each, ironically, has today drawn public anger not upon those working in the rehabilitative disciplines, but upon very visible judges few of whom, if any, purport to be competent in any rehabilitative skill. Indeed, it is an anger that has a sharp edge, for though judges observe a traditional silence when accused of failing to rehabilitate the imprisoned, judges nevertheless have legislatively or constitutionally been drawn within the range of public attack in other areas of the rehabilitative ideal—sentencing discretion, the indeterminate sentence, probation, parole, and prison conditions.

Notwithstanding that the rehabilitative ideal never actually dominated the criminal justice system as a value prior to punishment and deterrence, it was generally believed by the public and the Bench that it had that primacy. In any case, substantial defections from that ideal began in the 1960's, not only among editorial writers and politicians but among scholars as well. Today, the ideal is incanted solemnly at sentence, but even then neither Bench nor counsel discuss it.

Why has the rehabilitative ideal depreciated so sharply?

The answer must be traceable to ideas that drain belief in the notion of the mutability of human character and behavior. I will point to several of them.

The Collapse of Public Order

The nineteenth century belief in the simplicity and perfectibility of human nature has been profoundly shaken by the Freudian [Austrian psychoanalyst Sigmund Freud] revolution, to say nothing of the unprecedented savagery of the twentieth century. There is in America a continuing and almost apocalyptic increase in crime, notwithstanding that our average sentence is the longest in the Western world. Inevitably, a sense of helplessness, a foreboding of a collapse of public order is present at every dinner table. As for confidence in the utility of traditional therapeutic means, it has all but vanished. Indeed, it is generally accepted that a rehabilitative technique of any kind is yet to be discovered. Belief in the power of the public educational system to perform its simplest objective has been lost, hence the claims of education are not received as once they were. There has been a profound depression in the structure and authority of the family, and with it a decline of those family virtues associated with rehabilitation. A pervasive pessimism, an almost open contempt, for government has seeped into the public mind. A new mentality has arisen, markedly anti-intellectual in orientation, disclosing in American culture a sense of dependency, a seeking out of comfort and self-awareness, a flight from pain and personal responsibility. Moral passion has not declined. It has disappeared. These social facts are fragments of deeper changes which strikingly distinguish the major political movements of the twentieth century from those of the nineteenth. As Isaiah Berlin has observed, two devastating elements, traceable to Freud or Karl Marx, have united in the political movements of the twentieth century. One is the idea of unconscious and irrational influences that outweigh reason in explaining human conduct. The other is the idea that answers to problems exist not in rational solutions but in the extinguishing of the problems by means other than thought. So it is that the rehabilitative ideal, congenial to the essentially intellectual age of reform of the early 1800's, has depreciated with the twentieth century's devaluation of the intellect and the will. Looking back over the past two centuries, we see that science, as a new way of knowing, not only promised to augment man's power but dramatically delivered on that promise. The power it delivered, however, proved to be over nature only. It did not increase our power over ourselves to become better people. It has left man unchanged, sitting, as it were, in the evening of his life in a warehouse filled with his technology.

Punishment for Habilitation

Punishment is not antithetical to habilitation; rather, punishment or the threat of punishment is essential to habilitation. Offenders generally do not walk in off the streets voluntarily asking to participate in a demanding program to change their thinking. Moreover, offenders do not change when they are absolved from consequences and are free to do as they please.

Stanton E. Samenow, *Straight Talk About Criminals*, 1998.

We are thus living at a critical point in the shaping of an American penal policy. We could increase penal sanctions by matching brutality for brutality, but ethics and utility argue against it. In any case, a political consensus fortunately does not support what is essentially a regressive, primitive gesture. Equally without a political consensus are programs for social reforms directed at what some think to be causes of crime—unemployment, racial discrimination, poor housing. Whether such conditions cause crime is disputed and, in any case, a penal policy is too narrow a platform upon which a plan of social reform can be based.

In my opinion, the most desirable penal policy is that of just punishment, the swift punishing of blameworthy behavior to the degree of the offender's culpability. By such a policy we reaffirm the reality of moral values. Thus we answer those who challenge the conception of man's moral responsibility. Thus we create hope in a future based upon ancient moral truths from which so many have drifted into a night of philosophical neutrality.

The Idea of Just Punishment

The idea of just punishment has a wide consensus. It is a statement of a natural, moral intuition. It declares the moral autonomy of man without which all value systems are bound to be anarchic. It recaptures the lost community of moral and legal elements which once characterized crime and punishment, and without which a society loses its stability. As for the rehabilitative ideal, it should be stripped of its pretentiousness, if not of its very name. It is a hope of changing behavior, and nothing more. It is a goal, not a reality. In prison it should be directed at objectives that can be realized, particularly the avoidance of the deformative influences of prison life. Efforts at rehabilitation might well be concentrated at the offender outside of the prison setting, the one place where rehabilitation might have a fair chance of accomplishment. Surely rehabilitation is unlikely in prisons in which minimum standards of personal safety, health, and humane treatment are often violated. Indeed one cannot leave the literature of penology without the conviction that, if he were required to design a place in which the behavior of a man could never be improved, he would draw the walled, maximum security prison, very much like those into which men were led for rehabilitation in the early 1800's and are kept until this very day.

This time in which we live need not be an age of cynicism and despair. There is no principle that compels us to accept the philosophical debris of history. This time can, if we would but will it, be an age in which the fixed human values of Western civilization are brought back into their natural ascendancy. They who believe that man is not truly free, and hence not truly responsible, who market man as a rational animal without free will, who recognize neither good nor evil but only what is personally useful or harmful, who find the rule of right and wrong only in the current opinion of men, all these are strangers in the West. The values of Western civilization are ultimately the standards of men who hold themselves accountable for their moral acts. Upon that accountability all social institutions rise and fall.

> *"Either we rehabilitate as many of these individuals as we can, or we pay a heavy price in both public treasury and human misery."*

Prisons Should Rehabilitate Inmates

Katarina Ivanko

In the following viewpoint, Katarina Ivanko argues that the main objective of prisons should be to rehabilitate inmates. Ivanko contends that crime is a complex problem and should not be met with the singular and simple solution of incarceration. She claims that too much responsibility is being placed in the hands of correctional workers, and that families, churches, and communities need to do more to help rehabilitate criminals and prevent recidivism. Ivanko is a mental health worker at the Ohio Department of Rehabilitation and Correction.

As you read, consider the following questions:
1. In Ivanko's opinion, how does public opinion set back the movement for rehabilitation?
2. How does the author support her view that crime is a "complex dilemma"?
3. According to Ivanko, what factors contribute to recidivism?

Reprinted from "Shifting Gears to Rehabilitation," by Katarina Ivanko, *Corrections Today*, April 1997. Reprinted with permission from the American Correctional Association, Lanham, MD.

There is a real perception that America's crime rate is spiraling into crisis. Not only is the prison population dramatically rising, most Americans believe that our streets are becoming more unsafe. Between the talk shows and columnists, we are led to believe that the moral fabric of our society has so decayed that our future is predictably bleak. During the thick of [the 1996] political campaign season, we were bombarded with sound bites and slogans that reinforced our worst fears. As a result, the American public has adopted a simplistic viewpoint on crime with an even more simplistic solution: "Lock them all up."

Crime in the New Millennium

Despite public sentiment to lock up the entire criminal element in our society in costly new prisons, this cannot and will not occur. Crime is not something that can be eliminated by creating a criminal underclass that is incarcerated and forgotten. Consider that more than 5.3 million American adults are under some form of correctional supervision, with just over 1.5 million behind bars, more than at any other time in our history. Demographics experts and criminologists tell us that the worst may still be ahead, with the incidence of juvenile and young adult crime expected to rise as we approach the new millennium.

How, then, do we reconcile these ever-increasing crime rates with record rates of incarceration? Is there some threshold or critical mass in the number of incarcerated people that we must achieve in order to make a difference? Isn't "locking them up" working?

A Complex Dilemma

As a mental health worker with the Ohio Department of Rehabilitation and Correction, I have observed first-hand the complex dilemma that we desperately hope will just go away. I also am a taxpayer who asks whether we are simply burying our heads in the sand in the hope that the crime problem will somehow resolve itself. We all ask the same questions: What does the future hold for our children? What can I do to make a difference?

While there seems to be a great deal of information available on the prevalence of crime in America, there is very little in the way of understanding, and even less in the way of solutions. We tend to look for people to blame or assume responsibility when we should be looking for the origins and reasons behind these spiraling crime rates in our cities and towns.

Maintaining Humanity

California did a seven-year recidivist rate study and found a dramatic drop in the recidivist rate of these inmates [who had participated in arts programs] after they left prison, compared to the general prison population. These people did not commit crimes when they got back into the free world. Something really profound had happened to them in the prison setting that transformed their behavior. So you can also make the argument that you're reducing crime on the outside by bringing these programs in.

When a guy comes up to me and says, "Why should I be paying for music lessons for some convict when I can't afford it for my own kids," I say, it just makes the world a little safer for your kids. Yes, your kids should have art lessons. Everyone should have art lessons. But these programs pay for themselves and they represent a significant benefit to the community at large. These people come back out. Ninety-five percent of the people who go into prison come back out. And how do you want them to come back out? Do you want them to be bitter and angry and hostile? Or do you want something in place that maintains their humanity and keeps the human side alive? This is the most compelling argument.

Grady Hillman, interviewed by Steve Durland, *High Performance*, Spring 2000.

Research data clearly shows no correlation between the incidence of crime and the rate of incarceration. That is, crime has swelled in our country despite the high level of incarceration. Society insists that individuals accept responsibility for their behavior, yet there is ample proof that nearly every segment of society shares an element of blame: broken families, failed schools, failed churches and temples and the failure of community support mechanisms.

And we in the corrections industry legitimately ask: How can we be expected to single-handedly repair all the damage that has taken place? We can't. If a man or woman comes from a dysfunctional family, has little education, no medical care, no job or job prospects and no ongoing drug or psychological counseling, can we honestly expect him or her to avoid falling into the abyss of recidivism?

Renew Our Focus

The overwhelming majority of convicts one day will be released and their public privileges restored. Putting our heads in the sand and ignoring these men and women will only ensure recidivism. In short, either we rehabilitate as many of these individuals as we can, or we pay a heavy price in both public treasury and human misery.

Correctional workers are expected to perform this miracle of rehabilitation. And we try our best to help individuals who, by the time they enter prison, are broken from so many years of failure. But we need the support of families, schools and churches. To truly rehabilitate the criminal element in our society, shouldn't we start focusing on what they're going home to? It is time to renew our focus to discover what else can be done besides "locking them all up."

> *"Supermax facilities . . . have an established track record of success as pressure-release valves for overburdened systems."*

Violent Offenders Should Be Placed in Supermax Prisons

Jessica Gavora

The super maximum security prison—or supermax prison—is a recent trend in the American penal system. Supermaxes are separate, highly controlled facilities designed to house inmates that are too violent to be held safely in the general prison population. In the following viewpoint, Jessica Gavora describes one such program in Maryland. Supermax prisons are effective, she argues, because they protect other inmates and prison staff. She opposes federal efforts to restrict their use. Gavora is the director of the New Citizenship Project, a nonprofit public policy group.

As you read, consider the following questions:
1. According to Gavora, what are the three types of offenders housed in Maryland's supermax prison?
2. What "constitutional rights" of inmates were allegedly being violated in Maryland's supermax?
3. According to the author, how has the rate of murder among inmate populations changed since the introduction of supermax prisons?

Reprinted from "Maryland's Prison of Last Resort," by Jessica Gavora, *The Washington Post*, August 25, 1996. Reprinted with permission from the author.

The 288 most dangerous men in Maryland are incarcerated in "supermax," the Maryland Correctional Adjustment Center.

Supermax is one of a growing number of security facilities that take the worst of the worst—murderers and rapists who have continued their violent behavior while incarcerated—and lock them away in a redoubt of fortified walls and high-technology surveillance equipment. Supermaxes isolate "bad" prisoners from the general population and incorrigibles from one another.

For the Safety of Inmates

Maryland's highest security prison houses three kinds of inmates: "serious institutional rule violators" (typically inmates who have assaulted or killed guards or other inmates), serious escape risks and prisoners awaiting death sentences. In all, 105 murderers and 19 rapists spend their days in Maryland's supermax in what the corrections system calls "restricted confinement."

Inmates are alone 23 hours a day in their 65-square-foot concrete cells. Meals are passed through narrow slits in solid metal cell doors. Out-of-cell time is spent alone, too, in a windowless dayroom.

"When we were letting them rec [recreation] together they were killing each other, so we had to stop," said William Sondervan, Maryland's assistant commissioner for security operations.

Despite such concern for the safety of inmates—not to mention the prison staff—the Clinton Justice Department now is insisting that the isolation of inmates at supermax is cruel and unusual punishment. Deval Patrick, assistant attorney general for civil rights, is threatening to sue Maryland for alleged violations of prisoners' civil rights.

Questionable Violations

Each year, the 50 states spend $81 million defending themselves against prisoner lawsuits seeking redress for civil rights "violations" ranging from insufficiently stylish foot-wear to faulty television reception. This epidemic of prisoner litigation—one-fourth of the civil cases filed in federal trial court in 1995 were initiated by prisoners—is complemented by federal judges who impose "voluntary" consent decrees on states. In 1990, 1,200 state prisons were operating under judicial edicts covering everything from inmate population caps to how many electrical outlets each cell must have.

The effect of this litigation explosion has been to greatly circumscribe the control of states over their own prison systems. Some states have passed legislation curbing prisoner lawsuits, but attorneys general from Tallahassee to Phoenix looked to Congress for federal relief. Congress responded in 1996 by passing the Prison Litigation Reform Act.

For Law and Order

My father, whose second career (following military service) was as a correctional officer, saw [the] deterioration of law and order within the prison. . . . As he pulled duty as captain of the evening shift, he had ordered a violent prisoner into isolation, not once, not twice, but three times. Each time, the prison psychologist released the prisoner back into the population the next day. The third time the prison psychologist released the prisoner back into the population, that prisoner killed another prisoner. My father said, what did the dead prisoner do to deserve being killed. Obviously, being a convict, the dead man was guilty of something, but whatever that was, he had received his sentence, and was repaying his debt to society.

Clifford F. Thies, *St. Croix Review*, December 1998.

The legislation, which forces prisoners to pick up the tab for lawsuits and limits the ability of judges to impose consent decrees, was signed by Clinton as part of a larger spending bill on April 24. But the ink had barely dried on Clinton's signature before his Justice Department stepped in to replace the liberal federal judges and legal-savvy convicts whose meddling in state prison systems had been curtailed by the legislation.

In a May 1, 1996 12-page letter to Gov. Parris Glendening, Patrick charges that Maryland's supermax prison is violating inmates' constitutional rights through a range of offenses from inadequate exercise equipment to lukewarm meals. He gives the state 49 days to comply with a three-page list of "necessary remedial measures" or be prepared to face a federal lawsuit.

Track Record of Success

Thirty states, the federal government and Canada all have supermax facilities. These prisons have an established track record of success as pressure-release valves for overburdened systems. In the 1970s, before the advent of supermax prisons, one out of every 1,200 prisoners in the California system was murdered by a fellow inmate. Today, that rate has shrunk to one in 12,000.

Nevertheless, Maryland officials say federal civil rights investigators seem to believe that the facilities by their very existence are cruel and unusual punishment, a violation of the Eighth Amendment. This, even though Patrick admitted in his letter that he was "unable to find evidence of a pattern of physical abuse by supermax staff against inmates."

What Patrick did claim to find, however, was a host of violations of prisoners' "rights." Among them were the "rights" to outdoor exercise, piping hot meals and daily visits by medical personnel.

The Standoff for Supermaxes

In a sharply worded rejoinder, the Maryland attorney general's office told Patrick that his charges reflect his civil rights division's "philosophical opposition to 'supermaximum' facilities without regard to constitutional criteria." It noted that the law allows the Department of Justice to redress only "egregious" constitutional violations, a standard, the attorney general's office argued, not met by Patrick's charges. The Department of Justice has yet to take action.

The timing of the investigation of supermax—coincident with the passage of the Prison Litigation Reform Act—is puzzling. As one Maryland official said, "The Prison Litigation Reform Act really captures the national view of how people feel about prisons." Yet Maryland corrections officials find themselves in a standoff with federal officials over the future of the supermax prison. Unfortunately, they can't look to the Prison Litigation Reform Act for relief—it spares states from the tyranny of liberal federal judges and litigious inmates but not from the interference of federal regulators.

"What is dangerous is equating justice with punishment and believing that punishment (of others) is necessary."

Offenders Should Not Be Placed in Supermax Prisons

Mara Taub

In the following viewpoint, Mara Taub argues that punishment in supermax prisons violates human rights. She argues that methods used to detain offenders have no correctional value and amount to torture. Taub also claims that the majority of offenders placed in supermax prisons do not belong there, and the disproportionate minority presence in these prisons proves the prison system is racist. Taub is the director of the Coalition for Prisoners Rights.

As you read, consider the following questions:

1. According to Taub, how are offenders mistreated by guards at Wallens Ridge State Prison?
2. What is the "R.E.A.C.T. Belt System" according to Taub?
3. How does the author support her claim that most offenders in supermax prisons do not belong there?

Excerpted from "Super-Max Punishment in Prisons," by Mara Taub, *Resist*, January 2000. Reprinted with permission from *Resist*, 259 Elm St., Somerville, MA 02144.

We live in a time and country where more and more of us are being criminalized. Once criminalized, we are then demonized and held up as a threat to "the American way of life." We are being taught, over and over again, not to trust one another and to give up privacy rights in order to gain "security" or "convenience" or "savings." Those of us who used to think we lived in Athens must now recognize that we inhabit Sparta.

Super-maximum security prisons carry out this philosophy to the nth degree, with little public knowledge or accountability. Their existence is presented by the mainstream media as being regrettable, at best, but necessary.

What is dangerous to all of us now is the distribution of wealth and power in society—where some few people have too much of both and most of us have way too little of either. What is dangerous is creating a climate where many people support treating others in ways we would never believe we ourselves should be treated. What is dangerous is equating justice with punishment and believing that punishment (of others) is necessary.

Climate of Brutality

For three days in mid-November, I accompanied a New Mexico attorney to Wallens Ridge State Prison in far southwestern Virginia to serve as a notary. More than 100 New Mexico prisoners have been held in this facility since September, 1999. Even a visit to its climate of brutality was a chilling experience.

The prison administration refuses to allow the buildings or grounds to be photographed. The prison looks like a post-atomic holocaust science fiction space station situated on top of a dynamite-flattened Appalachian ridge. It is surrounded by two electrified fences and innumerable rolls of razor wire. Like so many prisons in the rural areas of our country, Wallens Ridge came into existence as the result of a local, community economic development effort.

Treatment of prisoners at Wallens Ridge has included a number of degrading "control" methods, including beatings upon arrival, and always features the routine use of racist language. People are strapped down, ankles, wrists and chest, when accused of rule infractions. They are kept that way for

48 hours, with guards taking bets on how long they will be able to refrain from wetting or dirtying themselves. Those accused of spitting on guards must wear muzzles.

Prisoners are required to wear devices around their waists officially called "R.E.A.C.T. Belt Systems" which are capable of delivering 50,000 volt shocks. According to an April 1999 *Human Rights Watch Report* concerning conditions at the twin super-max Virginia prison, Red Onion, "The extremely painful shock . . . has been described as 'resembling being hit on the back with a four-by-four by Arnold Schwarznegger.'" Prisoners are forced to stand, unmoving, away from a wall, while leaning on their noses against it. Night shift guards regularly walk along a row of cells hitting the metal doors. Visitors are not allowed to chat with each other while enduring long waits after long trips to see their loved ones. Even if repentance or remorse for past behavior were appropriate, such treatment inspires, if anything, exactly the opposite. Truly, survival with any kind of mental health is a triumph of the human spirit.

Worst of the Worst?

Who are these "worst of the worst" from New Mexico that supposedly need to be kept under such conditions? Many of these people are medium security prisoners, others are minimum; over three-quarters have less than five more years to serve, some only months. A number of them are experienced writ-writers—could that be a coincidence?

New Mexico prisoners were sent to Wallens Ridge in two batches, after a disturbance at a for-profit New Mexico prison during which a guard was killed. This was a prison the governor insisted could do "a better job for less money" than the state-run prisons. The New Mexico Department of Corrections itself says that the people they hold responsible for the death of the guard at Wackenhut Prison are currently being held in the state prison in Santa Fe. So why transfer these individuals to Virginia? Why so precipitously? Why transfer New Mexico prisoners who never were at the Wackenhut prison? And the worst part is, equivalent actions are being taken all over the country.

The manner in which human beings are being treated in

the Wallens Ridge super-max, as in super-maxes and control units throughout the country, is unconscionable. We do not become better people by calling names or being called names, by bullying or being bullied, by terrorizing or being terrorized, by holding others or being held ourselves idle and confined. Punishment produces hurting, angry and dysfunctional people. It is as harmful for those inflicting it as it is for those who receive it. It is dangerous for us all, as individuals, families and communities.

Retreating from the Free World

According to [psychology professor Craig] Haney, "You can go up to Pelican Bay [supermax prison in California] on any given day, and . . . there will not be a single visitor in the visiting room. It's 1,500 miles from southern California and, when you get there, your inmate is brought out in chains and put into a little booth. The only thing you can do is talk to him over a telephone and look through a great big, thick glass partition. You can't even touch their hand. And what happens is that these guys paradoxically retreat further and further into themselves, and so they discourage even the visitors who are willing to endure all of that, because they become very uncomfortable around people." Haney says that marriages dissolve and relationships with children wither. "The people with the worst prospects for successfully adjusting to the free world once they're released from prison are those who come out with nobody to rely on," he says. "These places are about as dysfunctional as you can imagine for providing them with the resources to make that transition work."

Spencer Harrington, *Humanist*, January 11, 1997.

To judge from the visiting room at Wallens Ridge, the majority of the 727 (as of November, 1999) prisoners in this 1,267 capacity prison who are not in protective custody are African American. Twenty-five percent of Virginia's population as a whole is African American. There are currently also 160 prisoners at Wallens Ridge from Connecticut, with several hundred more to come. The majority of them are Puerto Rican and African American. Virginia prisons also hold people sent from Delaware, the District of Columbia, Iowa, Michigan and Vermont. Such geographical range is not at all uncommon in these days of blatant trafficking in human flesh. At least 18 states send those they imprison to other states.

The United States is rare among countries in its extreme maltreatment by the people in power of so many of those without it. Others have found less brutal ways to deal with people regarded by those in power as problems. Even though the United States has signed a number of international treaties and covenants forbidding torture and the denial of human rights, such behaviors continue inside the US prison system. . . .

Mirroring the Ugly Truths

For many of the years since 1972 that I have been involved in prison/justice work, my activist-lawyer sister has repeatedly asked me: but why this issue? Because the police, the courts and the prison system of this country clearly show the contradictions between the rhetoric and the reality of our values. The country's punishment system exists as part of a larger whole.

Make no mistake about it: people and communities of color suffer most directly from the workings of the imprisonment system. The blatant racism is breathtaking. We must acknowledge the truth and the implications of the statistics. In 1993, 519 out of every 100,000 people as a whole were in prison. Of every 100,000 white people, 306 were in prison; whereas of every 100,000 African Americans, 1,947 were in prison. Even more stark, of 100,000 African-American males, 3,822 were in prison. These figures, of course, mirror the ugly economic truths of our country today.

We must join together, inform ourselves, and then, for however long it takes, loudly and publicly speak truth to power.

"Until . . . prison life becomes so much more unthinkably harsh than . . . the sweat of honest labor, crime will continue to escalate."

Prisons Should Not Coddle Inmates

Roger Stubblefield

In the following viewpoint, Roger Stubblefield argues that inmates are coddled in the current prison system. He claims that they have free access to services and amenities beyond the reach of many Americans. Stubblefield also asserts that inmates' needs are prioritized over those of citizens, and that this situation amounts to "cruel and unusual punishment" of ordinary people. Until life in prison becomes a truly undesirable option, he insists, crime will not be deterred by the threat of imprisonment. Stubblefield is a contributor to thepotatoe.com, a website that represents conservative opinions, and has contributed his writings to the *Houston Post* and the *Houston Chronicle*.

As you read, consider the following questions:

1. In Stubblefield's opinion, what is the role of the Eighth Amendment?
2. What examples does the author provide to support his argument that inmates have privileges many Americans cannot afford?
3. According to Stubblefield, what is the "criminal element"?

Excerpted from "Crime and Punishment," by Roger Stubblefield, *The Potatoe*, October 1999. Reprinted with permission from the author. Article available at www.thepotatoe.com.

The Eighth Amendment in the Bill of Rights prohibits, but does not define, cruel and unusual punishment. It would appear, then, that the definition of cruel and unusual was meant to be left to the sensibilities of society. One would, though, in today's America, be hard-pressed to make the claim that any criminal suffers from cruel and unusual punishment as the norm. That which is called punishment is far from being cruel and, in fact, any real punishment is unusual.

The Concept of "Hard Time"

Penalties for criminal activity range from simple fines and probation, for minor offenses, to the death penalty for capital crimes, with variations of lengths of imprisonment for median offenses. But how were criminals treated at the time the Eighth Amendment was penned?

In the late 1700's, public execution, by hanging or by firing squad, was the common method of carrying out the death penalty, a punishment exacted for heinous crimes. Prisons, penal institutions for lesser crimes, were harsh, cold and damp places, lacking any semblance of comfort.

Prisoners slept on piles of loose hay or straw mats. By day, prisoners were forced to hard labor in surrounding fields, rock quarries or mines. Insurrection or repeated disobedience was met with whippings with the lash or by floggings with wooden or cane poles. Individuals who underwent such correctional measures rarely needed a follow-up session. But some did live through it! Another, less severe behavioral modification consisted of being confined to a small box or cage for lengthy periods. Sometimes, a simple hole in the ground was an adequate substitute. . . .

While some may have found these punishments cruel, they certainly were not unusual. And the founding fathers did not see fit to abolish such punishments. In fact, for almost two hundred years after America's founding, these methods of dealing with the criminal element, save for some modifications, remained intact and acceptable. Electric chairs and gas chambers replaced the rope and the bullet. Prisoners were given cots to sleep on and more modern building techniques made prisons less cold and damp, but the concept of "hard time" remained.

Punishing the Innocent

Modern-day scofflaws and ne'erdowells experience far better treatment and conditions. Even the most monstrous of criminals are provided a life of ease and comfort. All are accorded a regimen of nutritious food, medical and dental care and exercise. Prisoners are no longer forced to work, at all.

Provided to them, free of charge, are exercise rooms with state of the art equipment, cable television, basketball and tennis courts that would rival any at the local "Y". They are provided recreation rooms with Ping-Pong and pool tables. They have access to computers and libraries with up-to-date law books, which are indispensable in constructing legal briefs for suits against transgressions by the penal system....

Chuck Asay. Reprinted with permission from Creators Syndicate.

Admittedly, prisoners—excuse me, that should read "inmates"—are still confined. Well, except when they're on a work release or a weekend furlough. And they do still serve time. Except when they are transferred to a halfway house or gain early release. But terms such as "bustin' rocks" and "chain gangs" have been replaced with "rehabilitation" and "anger management". Oh, and "prisons" are now "correctional facilities". And current criminals, by comparison, do not experience any personal affronts that could in any way be prohibited by the Eighth Amendment.

Cruel and unusual punishment still occurs, though, on the opposite end of the spectrum. There's that elderly couple across the street—the ones who have bars on the doors and windows of their home and are afraid to venture outside. And then there's the neighborhood children, whose lives are endangered simply by playing in the front yard or attending school. And there's those folks downtown that sleep on the floor in the back of the house or in the bathtub to avoid stray flying bullets.

These people—innocent, law-abiding citizens, all—know first hand about cruel and unusual punishment. They experience it daily, yet have done nothing to deserve it! If it is the sensibilities of a society that are to define cruel and unusual punishment, then it should be the sense of a society that should determine that consideration for the guilty must never take precedence over consideration for the innocent. However, that doesn't seem to be the case.

Suppressing the Criminal Element

There is a primitive, universal and insuppressible instinct in the animal kingdom, which also includes human beings, that promotes a drive to satisfy wants and needs with the least possible amount of pain and effort. In the human species, this drive, coupled with intelligence, can be beneficial and is responsible for mankind's advancement. . . .

Unfortunately, this selfsame drive, improperly channeled, produces the criminal element.

Methods for properly channeling this primitive drive towards constructive ends have long been known, written about and extensively detailed in ancient texts such as the Talmud, the Koran and the Bible. These ancient books contain the precepts of values, morals and simple good manners. It is these principles, or rather the adherence to these principles, that properly channel the drive more commonly known as human nature. . . .

People raised under these teachings and who believe in and maintain these principles develop a type of fail-safe mechanism, called a conscience, which sounds a mental alarm when boundaries are crossed. A conscience can be ignored, however, and, if ignored often, can cease to function. People who are ignorant of these guiding principles never develop a conscience or acquire a solid sense of right and wrong. It is these individuals, as well as those who successfully disregard the conscience, that constitute the criminal element.

The misdirected drive of human nature—that drive to satisfy wants and needs with the least amount of pain and effort—causes crime! But in the knowledge of the cause of crime lies, also, the ability for stopping crime.

For the criminal, it all boils down to a risk/reward equation. This is a well-known fact and a standard component of any homeowner's crime prevention pamphlet explaining how to make the risk side of the equation greater than the side for potential reward.

Until such time as the punishment of prison life becomes so much more unthinkably harsh than the day to day rigors of the sweat of honest labor, crime will continue to escalate. So, why, then, do we, as a society, afford the lawless greater access to amenities to which the average citizen would be hard-pressed to avail himself?

Prisons furnish a warm bed, three hot meals, entertainment and activities infinitely more favorable than any nonworking, non-earning individual could find living on the streets. Wage earners, from the lowest tier to the upper middle class, would find the combined costs for fitness centers, sports clubs, and medical and dental care (even with insurance) prohibitive. All are given free of charge to the convicted criminal! And we call this punishment?

Though "the enlightened ones" tell us it is a prerequisite of a civilized society, the sensibilities of this society, in trying to avoid any appearance of cruel and unusual punishment, have, instead, only succeeded in avoiding any appearance of good sense. We have lost sight of the intended purpose for punishment in the first place! It is not done for revenge; neither is it done for "rehabilitation". The purpose of punishment is, after all, to influence the risk/reward equation to the point where any actions of a criminal nature are just not worth the risk. Toward that, coddling criminals just doesn't cut it!

"A return to more-restrictive prisons will cause frustrations to erupt on both sides of the bars."

Prisons Do Not Coddle Inmates

Jess Maghan

In the following viewpoint, Jess Maghan claims the view that prisons coddle inmates is a popular misperception created by politicians who seek to make penal institutions more punitive. He argues that correctional managers need amenities in prisons because they work as effective behavioral tools, making prison environments less hostile. Maghan also contends prison managers, not politicians, know best what programs belong in today's prisons. Maghan is professor of criminal justice and director of the forum for comparative correction at the University of Illinois at Chicago.

As you read, consider the following questions:

1. In Maghan's opinion, what are the modern prison's surrogate roles?
2. How does the author support his argument that more restrictions in prison cause more prison violence?
3. According to Maghan, what factors make prison life dangerous?

Excerpted from "Why U.S. Prisons Should Keep the Barbells and TV," by Jess Maghan, *The Christian Science Monitor*, May 2, 1995. Revised in 2000 by the author. Reprinted with permission from the author.

As other forms of institutionalization decrease the *punishment paradigm*, with its emphasis upon increased use of prisons and greater penal austerity, has become the operative 21st century response to crime in the United States.

The safety and security of those inmates who seek to do their time and cooperate with institutional programs are jeopardized in the process of overarching efforts of maintaining overt custodial control of inmates. In the process, those inmates who seek to do "their time" and repair their lives are left on the sidelines. This population of inmates is seriously in need of primary focus. They, along with the correctional officers, are increasingly forced to survive within a security regime designed solely to control gang-bangers and troublemakers.

The trend continues with zeal at the State and local level of government to eliminate many program services to the nation's inmates. Everything from weight lifting and recreation to college education courses, drug counseling, cable TV—even smoking and coffee—are being eliminated as unnecessary for convicts and detainees in American jails and prisons.

This knee-jerk mentality assumes that hardening the environment will suffice to bring back punishment and penitence and to reform the repeat offender. Jimmy Cagney movies still live in the minds of those seeking change.

The Modern Prison's Surrogate Roles

Yes, every state and county in the land now has fully equipped, air-conditioned, and awesomely modern correctional centers. These new architectural wonders, often juxtaposed against aging court houses and other public buildings, provide an incredible array of correctional services for inmates: law libraries, gymnasiums, counseling and education, and so on. The comparison of these modern penal facilities to the poor conditions of most public schools and public recreational facilities in these communities is stark.

That these correctional facilities and their quality-of-life programs result from 30 years of litigation and the establishment of civil rights for incarcerated persons merely whets the appetite for returning these "new generation correction centers" back to punitive environments.

The fact that the current United States correctional system has a surrogate national public health role is too abstract for a public frustrated with the tough problems of crime. Corrections are becoming viewed as an unwelcome extension of public welfare and other public dole programs.

The traditional inmate program staff consisting of educators, chaplains, counselors, nurses, doctors, and psychologist is now fully complemented with an array of new staff: law librarians, inmate grievance officers, lawyers, legal aides and paralegal clerks, restorative-justice programmers, substance abuse counselors, AIDS counselors, parenting counselors, anger-management counselors, recreation supervisors, nutritionists, environmental health monitors, Occupational Safety and Health Administration (OSHA) supervisors, accreditation officers, affirmative action officers, public relations officers, lobbyists, construction and contracting officers, private sector prison liaison officers, and collective bargaining administrators. Will these professional inmate program staff survive?

The Responsibility of Correctional Managers

The traditional prison is now a complex prison—an interplay of exigencies and interests that leaves the simple relations of earlier days behind.

The intrusive surrogate and micro-operational authority within correctional agencies of federal special masters, compliance coordinators, and other oversight bodies have further cemented these changes in the correctional environment. The autonomy and authority of correctional administrators is at issue as never before. We now have several systems completing two decades of control under federal and special masters.

These situations have become counterproductive in all aspects. It is time to return these systems to the responsibility of their correctional managers. Only through ownership of the problems and solutions can any permanent change occur.

A Crisis of Control

There is a crisis of control in our correctional system. Gang warfare, turf disputes, racial tension, and institutional violence are rife. In this environment, a sudden withdrawal or change in inmate services may be disastrous. Criminal Justice Institute (CJI) reported 27,169 assaults committed by inmates and 14,903 assaults committed by staff in 1998. These tragic figures culminate with a further reporting of 38 line-of-duty deaths of correctional employees among 46 jurisdictions in 1998 and, not surprisingly, staff line-of-duty deaths and injuries are increasing in the 1999–2000 reporting period.

The Blows Keep Coming

The simple things I have lost would seem trivial to people outside of here. Even to me, much seems trivial. But taken as a whole and felt from the perspective of a prisoner, each loss is traumatic. I have lost my computer as well as the right to take educational classes and to buy health products such as protein powders and vitamins. My hot pot used for cooking healthful foods was banned. I have limited access to medical care and have recently been made to pay for soap, toothpaste, clothing, and privileges such as television and use of the gym—regardless of whether I use them. I feel almost constant uneasiness, not knowing where the next blow is going to come from or from what direction. But the blows do keep coming and seem to come harder and harder each time.

I have been in prison for seventeen years and have life without parole. I am supposed to be here forever. Living this life forever, with rules changing at the whim of any new official or angry legislator, is an experience that I have not come through unscathed. I feel that I cannot give up, but my actions seem to have little effect. Most prisoners like me have little gumption and much depression.

David Duhaime, Washington State Reformatory, *Friends Bulletin*, www.quaker.org.

In this environment, a sudden withdrawal or change in inmate services may be disastrous. To exacerbate this situation is sheer folly. Inmate idleness is one of the most lethal factors in maintaining control. With longer sentencing (resulting from "three-strikes" laws), overcrowding and limited work programs, a return to more-restrictive prisons will cause frustrations to erupt on both sides of the bars.

The Fragile Importance

The true political nature of American prisons is apparent in this dangerous situation. Prisons, reporting to the executive branch of federal, state, and local government, have always been prey to the ideology of the political majority. Politicians and their cohorts should spend a tour of duty with the correctional officers in America. They would rapidly grasp the fragile importance of some form of distraction from the mind-numbing din of the daily routine in our jails and prisons. Playing to the ignorance of an uninformed public, they are putting our whole nation at risk.

The quality-of-life program in American prisons raises important questions about the purpose and scope of incarceration: questions that can only be answered by social programs and other resources outside of prisons. Current philosophies and techniques of unit management, direct supervision, and related operational methods for delivering services to inmates will assume even greater industrial and programmatic proportion.

Rather than wax nostalgic for what were abysmal penal practices, politicians should focus on viable labor and behavior modification programs, like boot camps. These programs can complement public sector initiatives, restore deteriorating infrastructures, and restore the legal responsibility for citizens. Prisons should do less, not more, harm for both keeper and kept.

Periodical Bibliography

The following articles have been selected to supplement the diverse views presented in this chapter. Addresses are provided for periodicals not indexed in the *Readers' Guide to Periodical Literature*, the *Alternative Press Index*, the *Social Sciences Index*, or the *Index to Legal Periodicals and Books*.

James Brooke	"In 'Super Max,' Terms of Endurance," *The New York Times*, June 13, 1999.
Mark Frances Cohen	"Showdown with Sheriff Joe," *George*, December/January 2001. Available from 1633 Broadway, 41st Floor, New York, NY 10019.
William Glaberson	"Electric Restraints Use Stirs Charges of Cruelty to Inmates," *The New York Times*, June 8, 1999.
Ed Gogek and Jim Gogek	"Freedom Behind Bars," *San Diego Union-Tribune*, June 4, 2000. Available from 350 Camino de la Reina, San Diego, CA 92108-3003.
Alfred N. Himelson	"U.S. Prisons: Gulags or Country Clubs?" *World & I*, October 1997. Available from 3600 New York Ave. NE, Washington, DC 20002.
Jarvis Masters	"When Joyce Came to San Quentin," *Utne Reader*, September/October 1996.
David G. Morris	"Separate Some Prisoners So Others Have a Chance," *St. Louis Post-Dispatch*, February 7, 1999. Available from 400 S. Fourth St., Suite 1200, St. Louis, MO 63102 or www.postnet.com.
Patrica Puritz and Mary Ann Scali	"Civil Rights of Institutionalized Persons," *Corrections Today*, August 1998. Available from the American Correctional Association, 4380 Forbes Blvd., Lanham, MD 20706-4322.
Elizabeth Swasey	"Preference for Prisoners," *American Guardian*, January 1998. Available from the National Rifle Association of America, 11250 Waples Mill Rd., Fairfax, VA 22030-9400.
George Will	"Evidence Says Prison Fellowship Is Working," *Conservative Chronicle*, June 9, 1999. Available from PO Box 317, 9 Second St. NW, Hampton, Iowa 50491 or www.conservativechronicle.com.
John P. Zerillo	"Build the Minds, Not the Bodies, of Dangerous Inmates," *American Jails*, November/December 1997. Available from the American Jail Association, 2053 Day Rd., Suite 100, Hagerstown, MD 21740-9795.

CHAPTER 3

Should Prisons Use Inmate Labor?

Chapter Preface

In 1924, Arthur Davenport, chairman of the Advisory Committee on Prison Industries, stated, "The effect of placing on the open market a volume of goods that have been produced below normal costs is to lower prices and disorganize the market. . . . The increase in prison production, which is predicted, will exaggerate this evil." This sentiment toward inmate labor prevailed in the following decade. During the economic slump of the Depression Era, Congress outlawed the interstate transportation of products manufactured by inmates paid less than the minimum wage.

However, due to the recent prison population boom, Congress has established programs to bring private enterprise back into federal prisons. One estimation concludes that in the year 2000, correctional industries' sales would exceed $8 billion.

Supporters of inmate labor claim that inmate earning power is needed to subsidize the spiraling costs of the U.S. prison system. Moreover, they insist that giving inmates jobs structures their idle time, helps them to support their families, and reduces recidivism by giving them job skills and experience. Morgan Reynolds, director of the Criminal Justice Center at the National Center for Policy Analysis, asks, "Won't it be safer if they had some productive work experience, minimal job skills and a couple of thousand dollars saved up?"

Critics of inmate labor allege that private companies are tapping into the inmate workforces because they can exploit inmates by paying them lower wages than those earned by noninmates. They also assert most inmates come from economically challenged backgrounds, and making them accountable for prison costs aggravates their problems. While incarcerated, inmate James Thomas observed, "People who come to jail already lost everything. . . . This is just another thing to hold you back."

The issues discussed in this chapter deal with whether or not inmate labor is a viable solution to the challenges posed by an expanding correctional system and a growing prison population.

> *"We are giving these people a skill set so that when they do get out they are going to be productive."*

Inmate Labor Is Beneficial

Warren Richey

The modern prison system was based on Christian ideals, which originally included inmate labor. In the following viewpoint, *Christian Science Monitor* staff writer Warren Richey claims that the inmate labor system can have diverse benefits. He insists that inmate labor not only instills a work ethic in inmates, it can also make them accountable for rising prison costs, keep jobs in the United States, and boost the American economy. Ultimately, Richey contends that inmate labor gives inmates the rare opportunity to be part of a team, trusted and rewarded for their actions, and responsible for something other than their crimes.

As you read, consider the following questions:

1. What example does Richey provide to support his claim that inmate labor can give inmates marketable job skills?
2. How does Richey address the claim that prison labor is not beneficial?
3. According to the author, how can inmate labor bolster the American economy?

Reprinted from "Made in USA . . . but by Convicts," by Warren Richey, *The Christian Science Monitor*, January 14, 1998. Reprinted with permission from *The Christian Science Monitor*.

From the outside, Broward Correctional Institution doesn't look anything like a flourishing island of capitalistic enterprise.

Located beside the county dump at the edge of Florida's Everglades, the women's prison is ringed by 20-foot-high chain-link fences and coils of razor wire. Here, the state confines its worst female criminal convicts.

Some folks look at these inmates and see a collection of dangerous and uneducated misfits. Ron Gudehus sees something entirely different—potential.

For the past decade, Mr. Gudehus has transformed convicts into skilled employees who work at a full-service optical laboratory in the very heart of this maximum-security prison.

It is not make-work to keep prisoners occupied between meals. Broward Optical is a profitable business with real customers, real deadlines, real quality controls, and a bottom line.

Untapped Human Potential

Although controversial, the business activity here can help stanch the flow of US jobs to Mexico, the Caribbean, and other cheap labor markets overseas, say some economists and officials. They advocate doing on a national level what Gudehus is doing at Broward Correctional—seeing the country's 1.2 million inmates as potential national assets, rather than liabilities.

Currently, only 1 in 10 prisoners in the US works for pay. But they receive low wages—what prisons are willing to pay. That's usually well below the minimum wage.

But for the 2,400 inmates who work for the private sector—like those at Broward—pay is much better. They get the prevailing wage for products they produce. In Connecticut, that means the baseball caps used every year in the Little League World Series. In South Carolina, it's graduation gowns, cables, and furniture. And in Arizona, women prisoners are hired to take hotel reservations.

"There is just an awful lot of untapped human potential there," says Morgan Reynolds, an economist at Texas A&M and a fellow at the National Center for Policy Analysis in Dallas.

With the prison population reaching record highs and US

unemployment at record lows, Mr. Reynolds and other analysts are asking whether a large concentration of available workers in prisons might help keep US manufacturing and other jobs in the US.

When GEONEX, a computer mapping company based in St. Petersburg, Fla., was competing for a major project for an international telephone company recently, executives considered hiring workers in Pakistan or India to input computer data.

The Objective of Correctional Industries

One of the best descriptions of the objective of prison industries is from the Virginia Correctional Enterprises: "Prison should be a place no one wants to go, yet it must not be a place entirely without hope. For a few hard workers, there is an opportunity—an opportunity that must be earned . . . A regular work schedule, accountability and teamwork are foreign concepts to many inmates. . . . Correctional industries represents our one chance to instill responsibility, discipline and a sense of accomplishment in those who need it most."

James A. Gondles Jr., *Corrections Today*, October 1999.

But they went instead to Liberty Correctional Institution near Tallahassee, where today American prisoners are performing the work. In addition to training and a regular paycheck, some 80 inmates on the project can expect at least a $25,000-a-year job doing similar work when they are released.

"We are giving these people a skill set so that when they do get out they are going to be productive," says Kenneth Mellem, president of GEONEX.

Developing a Work Ethic

Reynolds says the vast majority of prisoners would gladly work for a paycheck if given the opportunity.

Sylvia Kee agrees. Ms. Kee, who is serving a life prison sentence, has worked at Broward Optical for 12 years. She is one of only 54 inmates employed in the 14-year-old business. But she says 90 percent of the 600 inmates at her prison want to work in the optical lab. It is the only program of its type in the prison.

But the use of prison-based labor for private enterprise is

controversial. Labor union officials and some industry groups say prison-based industries result in unfair competition and take jobs from law-abiding workers. Some critics call it a new form of slavery and warn of the establishment of American gulags.

The prison industries movement "uses incarceration as the remedy of choice for poverty, unemployment, poor education, and racism," writes Paul Wright, a prisoner in Washington State and editor of *Prison Legal News*. "If you've lost your job in manufacturing, garment or furniture fabrication, telemarketing or packaging, it could have simply been sentenced to prison."

Advocates of employing and paying inmates counter that the current system of human warehouses does little to prepare prisoners to make honest livings upon release. Learning a trade like lensmaking or computer data input, and being paid a regular wage, are far different than earning 15 cents an hour to mop prison floors or wash prison dishes, they say.

"If you can help people develop the right kind of attitude about work—a healthy, positive work ethic—it will go a long way in helping them once they get out," says Pamela Davis, president of PRIDE Enterprises, a nonprofit firm that promotes and runs prison industry programs throughout Florida. Broward Optical is a division of PRIDE.

The Economic Rewards

To prevent adverse impacts on workers outside prison, most prison-based businesses are restricted by law to supplying products only to public agencies. In a few cases, prison-made products and services may enter broader markets when they don't directly compete with other existing businesses.

Reynolds says the best answer to critics' concerns about prison labor would be to permit open competition to employ inmates. Those companies willing to take the risks and train the inmates should reap the economic rewards. At the same time, he says, inmate wages would be bid up, reducing the gap between in-prison wages and non-prison wages.

Reynolds calculates that if half of all prisoners worked in market-type jobs for five years, earning $7 an hour in full-time employment, they could boost the nation's gross domestic product by $20 billion. Prison-based industries would have a ripple effect in their communities, as they tap local suppliers and other services, advocates say.

Inmates who work contribute as much as 80 percent of their earnings to pay room and board at prison, family support, and taxes. They also pay restitution to crime victims.

For many, their prison jobs are the first time in their lives they've been members of a team, given responsibilities, trusted, and rewarded for jobs well done.

In a way it is a little taste of freedom. "I feel like when I am on the job I leave the prison out there," says Kee. "I always know where I am," she adds quickly, "but when I come in here I come in to give them the best of myself."

"The prison labor system does away with statutory protections that progressives and unions have fought so hard to achieve over the last 100 years."

Inmate Labor Is Not Beneficial

Gordon Lafer

In the following viewpoint, Gordon Lafer argues that inmate labor today sets the work reform movement back an entire century. Lafer asserts that inmate labor does little for the betterment of inmates' lives. He claims that inmate labor exploits inmates for capital gain and undermines the jobs and wages of ordinary workers. Lafer is an assistant professor for the Labor Education and Research Center at the University of Oregon and a member of the National Coordinating Committee of Scholars, Artists and Writers for Social Justice.

As you read, consider the following questions:

1. In Lafer's opinion, what makes a prison workforce desirable to private companies?
2. How does Lafer support his argument that inmate labor does not prepare inmates for re-entry to society?
3. According to the author, who is for and against inmate labor? Why?

Excerpted from "Captive Labor: America's Prisoners as Corporate Workforce," by Gordon Lafer, *The American Prospect*, September/October 1999. Reprinted with permission from *The American Prospect*, vol. 10, no. 46. The American Prospect, 5 Broad St., Boston, MA 02109. All rights reserved.

When most of us think of convicts at work, we picture them banging out license plates or digging ditches. Those images, however, are now far too limited to encompass the great range of jobs that America's prison workforce is performing. If you book a flight on TWA, you'll likely be talking to a prisoner at a California correctional facility that the airline uses for its reservations service. Microsoft has used Washington State prisoners to pack and ship Windows software. AT&T has used prisoners for telemarketing; Honda, for manufacturing parts; and even Toys "R" Us, for cleaning and stocking shelves for the next day's customers.

During the past 20 years, more than 30 states have enacted laws permitting the use of convict labor by private enterprise. While at present only about 80,000 U.S. inmates are engaged in commercial activity, the rapid growth in America's prison population and the attendant costs of incarceration suggest there will be strong pressures to put more prisoners to work. And it's not hard to figure what corporations like about prison labor: it's vastly cheaper than free labor. In Ohio, for example, a Honda supplier pays its prison workers $2 an hour for the same work for which the UAW has fought for decades to be paid $20 to $30 an hour. Konica has hired prisoners to repair its copiers for less than 50 cents an hour. And in Oregon, private companies can "lease" prisoners for only $3 a day.

But the attractions of prison labor extend well beyond low wages. The prison labor system does away with statutory protections that progressives and unions have fought so hard to achieve over the last 100 years. Companies that use prison labor create islands of time in which, in terms of labor relations at least, it's still the late nineteenth century. Prison employers pay no health insurance, no unemployment insurance, no payroll or Social Security taxes, no workers' compensation, no vacation time, sick leave, or overtime. In fact, to the extent that prisoners have "benefits" like health insurance, the state picks up the tab. Prison workers can be hired, fired, or reassigned at will. Not only do they have no right to organize or strike; they also have no means of filing a grievance or voicing any kind of complaint whatsoever. They have no right to circulate an employee petition or newsletter, no right to call a meeting, and no access to the press. Prison labor is the ultimate flexible and disciplined workforce. . . .

Troubling Developments

In Oregon in 1994, voters approved a ballot measure mandating that all prisoners work 40 hours per week and requiring the state to actively market prison labor to private employers. After only a few years, the new law has wrought dramatic effects. Thousands of public-sector jobs have been filled by convicts, while private-sector workers have been laid off by firms that have lost contracts to enterprises using prisoners. These troubling developments have prompted the state legislature to reconsider the wisdom of mandated prison labor. And the legislature is now debating whether to place a new initiative on the ballot at the next election that would allow voters to decide whether or not to undo the original initiative. The debate that is now unfolding will offer up a preview of the policy choices facing states across the nation as they confront what is fast becoming a significant threat to the job prospects of working Americans.

In Oregon the variety of jobs performed by prisoners is remarkable. Convicts are now responsible for all data entry and record keeping in the secretary of state's corporation division. They also answer the phones when members of the public call with questions about corporate records. Across the state, public agencies are using prisoners for desktop publishing, digital mapping, and computer-aided design work—all jobs that would otherwise be filled by regular public employees. . . .

Undermining the Workforce

Convict labor not only takes decently paid jobs out of the economy; it also undermines the living standards of those who remain employed by forcing their employers to compete with firms that use prisoners. The need to compete with poverty-level wages in the Third World has already undermined the bargaining power of American production workers. But until now, service jobs have proved very difficult to transport overseas. . . . [But domestic inmate labor] may force even service workers to compete at the level of the most impoverished overseas laborers.

Some proponents of prison labor argue that the practice either serves a rehabilitative purpose or helps prepare prisoners for re-entry into the workforce after incarceration. But expenditures for education and training have actually been declining. And even a cursory examination of how prison industries are administered makes clear that the motivation for these programs has little to do with rehabilitation. If training were one of the goals one might expect that workers would be selected for particular jobs based on their need for training. But there is seldom any selection process like this at work. And in those few cases where selection processes do exist, they are to help potential employees find convicts who *already* have skills needed for particular jobs. . . .

The Groups For—and Against—Prison Labor

Oregon's prison labor law was approved by 70 percent of the voters, including many union members. Many of these early supporters now claim they were fooled: they never imagined that making prisoners contribute to their own upkeep would end up taking jobs away from people on the outside. But if voters were deceived, the activists who wrote and financed the initiative knew just what they were getting.

The prison labor initiative was not, as one might expect, the product of victims' rights associations or conservative community groups. The campaign was almost entirely paid for by a clique of conservative businessmen who have promoted a host of anti-worker initiatives over the past decade. . . . This same group has backed virtually all of the most aggressively antilabor proposals of the past decade, including regressive tax reform, cuts in unemployment benefits, attacks on public employee pensions, and a prohibition on using union dues for political action. The effects of prison labor on the normal labor pool are, therefore, not an unintended by-product of tough-on-crime politics. The antilabor agenda was the heart of the matter from the start.

On the other side, the threat of prison labor has mobilized a coalition of prison activists, progressive policy organizations, and black and Latino community groups. Ultimately, however, the outcome of this struggle will depend largely on the labor movement. Union members have the most to lose, and thus the strongest incentive to oppose prison labor. Theirs is also virtually the only organized movement capable of undertaking the fight; only trade unions have the experience, resources, and membership base to mount an effective campaign on this issue. In fact, the labor movement has a long history of leading the fight against convict labor. In 1891, the Tennessee Coal Company locked out all of its union workers for refusing to sign a "yellow dog" contract barring them from union membership; locked-out workers were replaced with convicts. Soon after, however, the state discontinued the practice of hiring out inmates when the mine workers stormed the prisons, released the convicts, and burned the prison to the ground. . . .

Reprinted with permission from Kirk Anderson.

Moreover, few union members are inclined to think of prisoners as potential political allies. Instead, while there is clear agreement that prison labor should not take jobs out of the free market, most are eager to guarantee that prisoners have it tough. In discussing alternate proposals, for instance, one union member suggested that convicts should be made to carry heavy boulders from one side of the road to the other, and back again: "work" that would not interfere with anyone else's job, but would ensure that prisoners suffered appropriately. . . .

To date, opponents of prison labor have focused primarily on the security problems posed by convicts working outside prisons. Union representatives and progressive politicians have often focused on the danger of, for example, allowing rapists and murderers to rake leaves in parks where children are at play. And public safety is a real concern. In seeking job placements, the state has continually expanded the range of work and public interaction deemed appropriate for convicts. More alarmingly, Oregon has begun to compromise security standards to make prison work crews more affordable. Under the current system, employers may "lease" a ten-inmate work crew for $30 per day. However, the cost of providing a corrections officer to oversee this crew is nearly $300 per day, and this cost has led many agencies to limit their use of work gangs. To put more prisoners to work, the Department of Corrections recently sought to cut operating costs by replacing corrections officers with less-trained but lower-cost civilian overseers.

Attacking Prison Labor

Undoubtedly, attacking the safety of the prison labor system may be a more immediately effective political approach than appealing for solidarity with inmates. But as the prison industry works out the kinks in its operation, these security problems will be progressively diminished. For instance, if Louisiana Pacific—one of the financial backers of the prison labor initiative—decides to lay off union workers and construct a sawmill on prison grounds, there is no security argument that will effectively prevent the project from going forward. Prison labor must be opposed on the more durable basis that it threatens free labor. . . .

Building a consensus not only against the extensive employment of prisoners but also against mandatory sentencing laws will be a slow and arduous process, but we must undertake it if we hope to stop the expansion of prison labor before it gets much further. A "free market" economy ought to have no place for a vast army of prisoners undermining the wages of working people.

"The idea is not to be cruel, but to have an appropriate punishment that will also serve as a deterrent."

Inmate Chain Gangs Are a Proper Form of Punishment

Jayce Warman

The return of chain gangs in America's prisons in recent years has sparked controversies about human rights and the effectiveness of the prison system. In 1995, Alabama reinstated the penal practice of chain gangs in its prisons. Many states followed suit in an effort to keep their own correction facilities up to par. In the following viewpoint, Jayce Warman proposes that a modified chain gang—as a work program strategy—has potentially widespread and lasting benefits for both inmates and communities in his home state of West Virginia. He claims that such programs can contribute to the rehabilitation of criminals, relieve taxpayers of the rising costs of imprisonment, deter crime, and improve the community. A form of punishment with this many benefits, he contends, should be used widely. Warman is an undergraduate student at West Virginia University.

As you read, consider the following questions:
1. In Warman's opinion, how can chain gangs rehabilitate prisoners?
2. How does Warman support her argument that chain gangs can deter crime?
3. How does the author argue that chain gangs today can be transformed into an appropriate, humane form of punishment?

Excerpted from "We Aren't Just Talking About Pounding Rocks into Pebbles Anymore . . ." by Jayce Warman, March 29, 1998, www.as.wvu.edu/~jwarman/paper2.htm.

"America's prisons were originally intended to be self-supporting. Today, with the absence of chain gangs, prison inmates are a huge drain on taxpayers, despite the millions of available hours of healthy, prime age labor they represent," [according to the National Center for Policy Analysis]. Chain gangs began in about 1885 with the chains being a substitute for the locks and bars of maximum-security prisons. A steel band was clamped on each of the prisoners' ankles and connected by a twenty-inch chain. Then a three-foot long chain was attached to the ankle iron or the connecting chain and hooked onto the prisoner's belt. At night, ten or twelve convicts were kept in steel cages and chained to the bars with only enough room to lie down in their bunks. The pick and shovel were the chief tools of the chain gang which worked ten to twelve hours a day, depending upon the season, under the supervision of guards and a captain who knew how to build roads. Today, with America taking a tougher stance on crime, chain gangs have re-emerged in the penal systems. States such as Alabama, Arizona, and Florida have started to use criminals in chain gangs. Not all inmates are selected for chain gang detail. Florida chooses from a pool of inmates that excludes all those convicted of first-degree murder, escape attempts, sex offences, and inmates with psychological or mental conditions that make it difficult for them to work. West Virginia should implement the use of chain gangs in both its penal and juvenile systems as a means of rehabilitation, as a means of offsetting the costs of keeping prisoners in jail, and as a means of deterring them from future crimes.

Geared Toward Rehabilitation

The most important result of using chain gangs in West Virginia would be their ability to help rehabilitate criminals. Alan Harland points out that "correctional rehabilitation can be defined as an intervention to reduce recidivism." However, most prison programs are fallible because they are geared toward anticipating abnormalities in prisoners. They intimidate the prisoners, causing them to have few feelings of self-worth without means for self-improvement. This negative punishment that occurs in prisons has the unintended effect of sabotaging society by turning out more

"A Little Extra Freedom"

More than three months into the chain gang pilot program [in Wisconsin], legislative sponsors and the Department of Corrections officials say it is going smoothly. And after a summer of picking up trash, harvesting vegetables and trimming trees, many of the chain gang participants are also giving their endorsement. . . .

"If you like working, this is the job to have," said inmate Lacey Bryant. "If you are inside, you are just cooped up. Out here, you get a little extra freedom."

John Welsh, *Wisconsin State Journal*, September 15, 1997.

criminals instead of fewer; weaker morality instead of firmer. A new chain gang system could help solve problems like this and serve to rehabilitate criminals while discouraging juvenile offenders. A "self-determinate sentence" should be implemented where offenders have the amount of time to serve figured in dollar amounts based on the crime. Then, they remain in jail until they complete their sentence and the victim and society are both repaid. This gives them goals and a feeling like they are actually getting somewhere. If inmates and juvenile offenders were allowed to work together on projects they would learn the values of teamwork and also achieve better feelings of self-worth when they saw the end result. Also, they should be assigned worthwhile tasks and jobs that will actually help to serve them better in society. Instead of pounding rocks they could be helping to build houses for the poor, and in place of picking up trash they could be learning how to build and repair roads, all of which pay good wages. Habitat for Humanity, a non-profit service organization that helps build houses for those less fortunate, would be well served by the use of inmates and juvenile offenders. This organization would be able to reach out to a larger number of people, and the workers would learn valuable skills and gain self-esteem as they saw themselves having a positive impact on people's lives. In order to make this work, proper time and effort in the training and care of prisoners must be taken to ensure the desired results. Enabling prisoners to be outside of the jail environment while serving their sentence will also help them adapt back to life in society. David Duffee writes that "people change through a manipulation of personal relationships. . . . Rehabilitation is a strategy that is divided into two parts where the personality is the dependent variable and the social interaction is assumed to change the individual." This will reduce the culture shock common after an extended prison term, which will then reduce the number of repeat criminals who have lost touch with society and seek to go back to jail because it is their familiar environment.

Chain Gangs as a Resource

Another important aspect of the use of chain gangs in West Virginia would be offsetting the cost of housing prisoners. With the national average of housing a criminal at $27,000 a year, that can get expensive, especially with no return. Florida, a state that does use chain gangs, ran an average cost of $17,500 in 1996–97 to house its male offenders. . . . Moreover, the use of prison labor will allow the completion of jobs at a lower price, faster. The implementation of self-determinate sentencing would also help to complement these practices by adding incentives for working harder and quicker. In the past, chain gangs have proven to be effective means of cost cutting. In 1926, inmates completed a road in North Carolina at the cost of $5000 per mile, while the State Highway Commission gave the conservative estimate of $7500 per mile. Considering the increasing costs of labor and materials today, we should use prison workers to help complete major jobs. For example, roads are government funded projects as well as most prisons, so why not use a resource we have already paid for and save some tax money? The job loss that would occur with the employment of inmates is inconsequential for a few reasons. There would be jobs created by the need to have supervision and training of the prison work crews. . . . The main reason for joblessness today is frictional unemployment, which is people changing from one job to another. . . .

An Effective Deterrent

The other advantage of employing chain gangs in West Virginia is that they serve as a deterrent to crime. Max Grunhut simply puts it as "prison labor is the essence of prison discipline." Some of the jobs that would serve as deterrents range from breaking rocks, shoveling muck off roads, picking up trash, cleaning graffiti, and digging graves. Alabama has employed a rock-breaking program limited to those who have had unsuccessful attempts at parole and have ended up back in prison. The inmates are required to work ten-hour days, resting every twenty minutes, with Saturdays and Sundays off. Arizona has also employed a "scared straight" system of using chain gangs to dig paupers' graves. While digging, the inmates are told that most of the victims have died of drug overdoses, alcoholism, or a homicide in order to show some of the jails' tough cases how they might end up without changes. . . . A prisoner, Larry Gardner, employed in Alabama's chain gang for only twenty-four days after a parole violation of drunk driving following an earlier armed robbery conviction said, "It has broken me. I do not intend on being back in here again." David Pluff, working in Arizona's "scared straight" program, says, "Working these graves makes you think. I want to get out, go back to school and go straight. I never want to be in jail again." Chain gangs are an effective form of prison labor that serves as a deterrent.

Appropriate, Not Cruel and Unusual, Punishment

Chain gangs would help to improve West Virginia because they can be used as a means of rehabilitation, offsetting some of the costs of keeping prisoners in jail, and as a deterrent. What makes this an even better idea is that the system has moved out of the stone age, meaning the inmates no longer need to be chained together to be controlled. Technological advances have made possible the use of a stun-belt. A stun-belt is a device capable of delivering an eight-second burst of fifty thousand volts that stuns a disorderly inmate from up to three hundred feet for up to ten minutes with no long term physical damage to the prisoner. This device requires less supervision and also allows inmates to move with less restriction so that they are more productive. . . . Florida decided to individually shackle their chain gang workers as a means to make them more effective. "More work is able to be accomplished if people are not chained together," said

Eugene Morris, a spokesperson for the Corrections Department. He also says that "the idea is not to be cruel, but to have an appropriate punishment that will also serve as a deterrent." If what Erik Wright said was true, that "it is man's view of himself as a lawful and responsible person that will deter crime," then we would have no need for a penal system. Clearly, this is not the case. In order to reach the point in society where we do think of ourselves in this manner other means must be implemented, such as chain gangs.

"Let there be no mistake about it, there is an unambiguous historical connection between chain gangs and slavery."

Inmate Chain Gangs Are an Improper Form of Punishment

Tracey L. Meares

Many people associate chain gangs with the abolished practice of African American enslavement. In the following viewpoint, Tracey L. Meares affirms this belief and argues that the use of chain gangs is a practice with racist roots. She also claims that it does not deter crime or reduce recidivism, is an expensive form of punishment that creates a gratuitous spectacle of shame, and threatens public safety. Finally, Meares contends that chain gangs are an outmoded form of punishment that should be replaced with more humane policies that provide inmates with education and rehabilitation. Meares is a contributor to *U.S. Catholic* magazine.

As you read, consider the following questions:
1. How does Meares argue that chain gangs today mimic yesterday's black slavery ?
2. According to Meares, how can chain gangs put public safety in jeopardy?
3. What is the author's view of imprisonment's purpose? How do chain gangs undermine this purpose?

Excerpted from "Let's Cut Chain Gangs Loose," by Tracey L. Meares, *U.S. Catholic*, July 1997. Reprinted with permission from *U.S. Catholic* magazine, Claretian Publications, 800-328-6515, www.uscatholic.org.

Imagine the following scene: It's a hot summer day. The sun is beating down on African American men. They are shackled to each other as they chop weeds for 12 hours. Armed guards and panting dogs watch intently over the chained men.

One may think that this imaginary scene is rendered in the sepia tones of history. It is not. Chain gangs, unfortunately, have become an increasingly common part of the American landscape.

Chain gangs are a reality in at least seven states, and they are imminent in several more. Moreover, chain gangs are not confined to Alabama, the self-proclaimed heart of Dixie, and other former states of the Confederacy. Wisconsin, Michigan, Iowa, and Maryland—Union states all—have decided to welcome displays of shackled prisoners along state highways.

The Historical Connection

Let there be no mistake about it, there is an unambiguous historical connection between chain gangs and slavery. Advocates of the modern chain gang in Southern states trade on this historical connection. Anyone who disagrees need only consider the comment of one Alabama roadside chain gang spectator: "I love seeing 'em in chains. They ought to make them pick cotton."

At the beginning of this century chain gangs were used as a mechanism to keep African Americans in voluntary servitude even after Emancipation. Southern judges commonly sentenced African Americans convicted of vagrancy (also known as unemployment) or loitering to time on the chain gang, where iron shackles were welded to an offender's ankles, and dogs, whips, and starvation were used liberally.

Nor was a chain gang sentence limited to those convicted of petty crimes. In many cases mere breach of a contractual obligation was enough for a chain gang sentence. Contract-enforcement laws directed primarily at African American farm laborers transformed labor contracts into slavery. These laws made it a criminal offense for a farm laborer to quit a yearlong job for a better job at a higher wage. African American laborers were forced to choose between working out the original low-wage contract or spending several months of forced, brutal labor on a chain gang where fatality was not uncommon.

Though contract-enforcement laws are now unconstitutional relics of the past, the racial disparities in state prison populations have not changed. African Americans comprise about half—in Alabama, Georgia, and Maryland well over half—of the incarcerated prisoners in almost every state that has sanctioned the modern chain gang. (Iowa, with an African American prison population of 25 percent, is a notable exception.) These numbers mean that slavery's image is an inescapable aspect of the return of chain gangs.

The obvious costs of resurrecting a punishment so intimately connected with American slavery clearly outweigh any benefit American citizens can expect to gain. Aside from the very clear problems associated with the historical symbolism of the chain gang, there is a more basic problem. No one can convincingly argue that chain gangs will effectively reduce crime.

An Unlikely Deterrent

Chain gang proponents often express a desire to make prison so awful that a prisoner would not ever consider coming back. One must wonder how many legislators have been inside a state correctional facility. Prison already is not a pleasant place, as anyone who actually has been inside one can attest.

Chain gang proponents also argue that the public humiliation of service on a chain gang will lower recidivism and may even deter law-abiding folks from considering a life of crime. This argument assumes that little-to-no humiliation is associated with going to prison—clearly a ridiculous idea. It is extremely unlikely that humiliating service on a chain gang will advance the deterrent value that we already obtain through imprisonment.

Adding chain gangs to imprisonment is not a cheap way to purchase an additional measure of deterrence. Obviously chain gang service does not make imprisonment any less expensive. Legislators who advocate chain gangs as a shaming penalty need to think again. If shaming penalties are useful at all, they are useful for their potential to serve as alternatives to incarceration. But chain gang advocates usually propose to apply chain gang service to those already incarcerated. No one discusses using chain gangs to make probation or community service more harsh. The legislators who propose chain gangs as shaming penalties are simply throwing more money at an already expensive program.

Out on the Chain Gang

The inmates on the job held a trash bag, swing blade or shovel with one hand and the chain with the other as they began making their way along the roadside in groups of five. Guards toting guns watched them, and guard dogs barked from nearby prison pickup trucks.

"It's an experience I will never forget. I hope and pray I don't never come back. I don't like the idea of being used as a political chess piece," said Dwayne Rowe, a 25-year-old inmate serving seven years for selling cocaine.

James Sears, a 30-year-old inmate serving time for a parole violation, described the experience as degrading, adding, "you can't even chain five dogs up on the side of a road without the Humane Society doing something."

Jay Reeves, *Union Leader*, May 4, 1995.

Chain gang service makes imprisonment more expensive while reducing the public's safety. We do not send offenders to prison simply to deter them from committing offenses when they are released. We send offenders to prison to incapacitate them and protect the public. Removing prisoners from the confines of prison walls and requiring them to work along roadsides increases the chances of escape, as Alabama learned in January 1996 when two prisoners escaped from a chain gang. The risk to the public from chain gangs could be reduced by making sure that only very "safe" prisoners (embezzlers?) are allowed to work outside the prison; however, most chain gang proponents would resist this approach. Proponents call for more harsh treatment of violent and repeat offenders as a measure to reduce crime and protect the public, but they simply cannot have it both ways. They can either decide to keep so-called "incorrigible prisoners" behind prison walls, or proponents can attempt to make punishment more harsh for these offenders by requiring them to work outside in chain gangs. The most sensible option is obvious.

An Anachronistic Punishment

Why is there such a rush by lawmakers to drag these anachronistic punishments to the 21st century when numerous studies indicate that high school education and vocational training of prisoners is directly correlated with lower recidivism rates? It makes little sense to invest in an untested, morally ambiguous plan when that money would be much better spent on programs that can prepare a prisoner for the life he or she will lead outside. A life that will require a released offender to have basic reading and writing and maybe even computer skills. A life that is extremely unlikely to require an offender to know how to break rocks or chop weeds by the side of the road.

Perhaps lawmakers might support a policy that combines sound research and political appeal. How about this idea: Let's chain all inmates to desks and force them to learn to read and write. How about a bill to require that all inmates receive a General Equivalency Diploma? Granted we wouldn't be able to gawk at inmates learning in a classroom—like we can when driving by prisoners shackled together on the highway.

True, we wouldn't be able to laugh at prisoners flexing their minds at their desks as we do now when humiliated criminals build up their muscles swinging picks at the taxpayers' expense. ("See, son, that illiterate prisoner sure is gettin' what he deserves, havin' to learn to read and all" probably isn't what chain gang proponents have in mind.) Of course, we wouldn't be able to have second and third chances at humiliating these recidivists because educated prisoners might actually become contributing citizens rather than repeat performers. But such an approach might actually reduce crime, which is what the push for chain gangs is supposed to be about.

Lowering recidivism rates, deterring crime, and allowing human beings to retain some semblance of dignity are the true goals of imprisonment. Humiliation of prisoners that depends on our country's sad history of enslavement of human beings is not. The argument against chain gangs is about more than preserving the humanity of prisoners. It's about preserving the humanity of the citizens of the United States. Every single one of us is degraded by the trend to bring back this ignominious punishment.

As Christians, we have an obligation to take a stand against morally outrageous punishments such as the chain gang. The gospels teach us to lead others by example, not to follow them blindly. It is time for us to move forward into the 21st century. It is time to repudiate chain gangs once and for all.

Periodical Bibliography

The following articles have been selected to supplement the diverse views presented in this chapter. Addresses are provided for periodicals not indexed in the *Readers' Guide to Periodical Literature*, the *Alternative Press Index*, the *Social Sciences Index*, or the *Index to Legal Periodicals and Books*.

Timothy Burn	"Prison Industry Grows as Inmate Population Swells," *Insight on the News*, March 1, 1999. Available from 3600 New York Ave. NE, Washington, DC 20002 or www.insightmag.com.
Daniel Burton-Rose	"Labor Held Captive," *Dollars and Sense*, May/June 1998.
Corrections Today	Special Issue on "Correctional Industries," October 1999. Available from the American Correctional Association, 4380 Forbes Blvd., Lanham, MD 20706-4322.
Peter Finn	"Putting Ex-Offenders Back to Work," *National Institute of Justice Journal*, July 1999. Available from U.S. Department of Justice, Office of Justice Programs, National Institute of Justice, 810 Seventh St. NW, Washington, DC 20531.
Eve Goldberg and Linda Evans	"The Prison-Industrial Complex and the Global Economy," *Turning the Tide*, Summer 1998.
Kirstin Downey Grimley	"Recruiting a Captive Audience," *Washington Post*, November 10, 1997. Available from 1150 Fifteenth St. NW, Washington, DC 20071.
Alex Lichtenstein	"Chain Gang Blues," *Dissent*, Fall 1996.
Christine Long-Wagner	"When Prison 'Jobs' Threaten Public Safety," *Shield*, Summer 1998. Available from Law Enforcement Alliance of America, 7700 Leesburg Pike, Suite 421, Falls Church, VA 22043.
Rod Miller	"Inmate Labor in the Twenty-First Century," *American Jails*, March/April 1997. Available from American Jails Association, 2053 Day Rd., Suite 100, Hagerstown, MD 21740-9795.
Stephen Nathan	"The Prison Industry Goes Global," *Yes!*, Fall 2000.
Marylee N. Reynolds	"Back on the Chain Gang," *Corrections Today*, April 1, 1996. Available from the American Correctional Association, 4380 Forbes Blvd., Lanham, MD 20706-4322.
Harry Wu	"Slaves to the State," *Index on Censorship*, January 2000.

CHAPTER 4

What Are the Alternatives to Prisons?

Chapter Preface

Many of America's prisons presently operate at or over full capacity. In an attempt to relieve the problem of overcrowding in U.S. prisons, many lawmakers, criminal justice professionals, and activists are calling for the use of alternative sanctions in the place of prisons. Proponents of alternatives to prisons suggest that nonviolent offenders should be diverted from prisons and managed under less expensive and intrusive modes of supervision.

Such alternative sanctions include parole, probation, drug treatment, halfway houses, creative sentencing, electronic monitoring, and "shock incarceration" (boot camp), each prescribing different levels of surveillance for offenders. One of the most popular of these alternatives is electronic monitoring. With electronic monitoring, an offender wears an electronic bracelet that sends signals back to a receiver placed in the offender's home. If he or she strays too far from the receiver during detention hours, the signal is broken and the receiver alerts a monitoring station. Supporters argue that electronic monitoring successfully punishes and rehabilitates nonviolent offenders by restricting their movements while allowing them to work and support their families. They also maintain that as technology advances, electronic monitoring will improve. For instance, an offender's whereabouts can be accurately tracked using recently developed satellite monitoring technology.

However, critics argue that electronic monitoring is not reliable and that offenders have committed violent crimes while being electronically monitored. For example, in 1999, a woman putting up curtains in her home in Annapolis, Maryland, was killed by a stray bullet fired by an electronically monitored drug offender, forty minutes before his curfew. And in 2000, a twelve-year-old girl in Anderson, Indiana, was raped and murdered by the sixteen-year-old boy next door under electronic arrest.

In the following chapter, various viewpoints will examine the benefits and disadvantages of the alternatives to prisons. These alternatives challenge contemporary ideas of how social order can be maintained.

"Fewer violations of parole . . . suggest that fewer ex-inmates are falling back into the cycle of drugs, violence and incarceration."

Parole Can Succeed as an Alternative

Neely Tucker

Not only has the U.S. prison population dramatically increased in recent years, so has the number of Americans on parole or probation, which reached a record high of 4.5 million in 2000. In the following viewpoint, *Washington Post* staff writer Neely Tucker contends that parole can succeed as an alternative to imprisonment. He claims that fewer ex-inmates are relapsing into cycles of crime. Key to keeping ex-inmates from returning to prison, he contends, are programs that assist them in rebuilding their lives when they are released. Tucker insists that services adopting a "social-work attitude" toward ex-inmates are most successful, such as job placement and anger management programs.

As you read, consider the following questions:
1. According to Tucker, how did the rate of parole violations in Washington, D.C. change between 1998 and 2000?
2. How does Tucker support his claim that programs to help ex-inmates are being revitalized?
3. According to Eric Lotke, quoted by the author, how have parole officers been successful in keeping ex-inmates out of prison?

Reprinted from "Out of Prison for Good, into a Life for Better: Growing Efforts Offer Ex-Inmates a Chance for Permanent Change," by Neely Tucker, *The Washington Post*, November 9, 2000. Copyright © 2000 by The Washington Post. Reprinted with permission.

Sundays you can find Charles Gantt at church. Weekdays, you can find him at his job, working with troubled children. Weekends, you can find him playing football with his two sons.

The one place you can't find him is prison, which is notable considering that Gantt, 31, has spent nearly a third of his life incarcerated in one facility or another. He's been convicted of assault with intent to kill. Assault with a deadly weapon. Dealing cocaine.

But today, Gantt is part of a quiet trend in the District [Washington, D.C.]—men who have been in jail who are turning their lives around. Though precise numbers are hard to come by, studies show that the percentage of ex-inmates from Washington who violate parole has dropped about 60 percent, from an average of about 150 violations a month in mid-1998 to 50 to 70 a month in November 2000.

Gantt, released in January 1998 and on parole until 2007, has been working one and sometimes two jobs since his release. His record is squeaky clean. His family and employers say he's an inspiration.

"I was making $5 per hour when I got out; now I'm making more than $13," said Gantt, the senior outreach coordinator for the Alliance for Concerned Men, a nonprofit group that works with ex-offenders and troubled youths. "I'm back with my kids. I'm in church every Sunday. I've got a car, an apartment and a girlfriend. In four or five years, things are going to be just that much better."

Leaving Crime Behind

Stories like Gantt's will be more important in the coming years, as a record 4.5 million Americans are now on parole or probation. In the District, which has one of the nation's highest rates of incarceration, about 10,500 people are on probation or parole.

Fewer violations of parole, while not ironclad evidence, does suggest that fewer ex-inmates are falling back into the cycle of drugs, violence and incarceration. That saves taxpayers money, decreases crime rates, reunites families and gives men like Gantt a reason to be optimistic about their futures.

Gantt's supervisor, Peter L. Jackson, said Gantt has pulled

off one of the toughest challenges for young men once caught up in crime—leaving the lifestyle behind.

"Charlie has done what very few guys in Lorton [Correction Complex in Lorton, Virginia] have been able to do, which is come out and stay out," Jackson said. "He's dedicated, works hard and does what he says he's going to do. He's the perfect example of someone coming out [of prison] and starting a new life."

Stories like Gantt's, though seldom the stuff of newspaper headlines, are profound examples of personal redemption. They also illustrate the way a combination of federal, city and private groups are trying to build a system that offers former inmates a realistic chance of success.

Revitalizing the Lives of Ex-Inmates

The Court Services and Offender Supervision Agency (CSOSA), a federal entity created in the 1997 Revitalization Act, has brought new life and new money into the District's troubled efforts to help former inmates. Drug Court, a program to help nonviolent offenders with addiction problems, has taken hold in Superior Court. And a number of grassroots groups have increased programs for ex-inmates, offering everything from a getting-out-of-prison guidebook to classes on controlling violent tempers.

In November 2000, CSOSA opened a "Learning Lab" at St. Luke's Center in the 4900 block of East Capitol Street, a program for inmates to get their general equivalency diploma and develop literacy and computer skills. And more than 100 city residents from a variety of professional backgrounds attended "Study Circles," a five-week series of meetings sponsored by the D.C. Prisoners' Legal Services Project, brainstorming for new ideas on how to help ex-prisoners.

"There's a new, almost social-work attitude of helping men and women who have been in prison," said Pauline Sullivan, co-director of Citizens United for Rehabilitation of Errants (CURE), a nationwide organization that works with former offenders and their families. "There are a growing number of programs and resources out there to help them make it."

That's a distinct change in the District.

The city's halfway house system was so badly run during

the mid-1990s, with hundreds of parolees escaping, that inmates at Lorton were no longer sent to any post-incarceration facility. Like Gantt, they were simply released from jail to the street.

"They only opened the gate wide enough for me to slip out sideways," Gantt said. "My family hadn't gotten there to pick me up yet. I was walking around in my prison jumpsuit."

For inmates with no families, there were few services to help restart their lives.

Few Win Parole in California

Parole for eligible inmates evaluated by the Board of Prison Terms has become all but extinct in California. A 1988 voter initiative gave the governor the power to block the parole of murderers. In cases involving other crimes, the governor can ask the board to reconsider a grant of parole. In those cases, the board usually reverses its earlier finding.

	Parole hearings	Parole grants	% of inmates approved for parole	Reversed by governor or returned to board for reconsideration
1979	515	96	19%	—
1989	1,266	45	4%	0
1999*	1,489	13	0.9%	13

*To date

Board of Prison Terms, *Los Angeles Times*, October 3, 1999.

"That was a formula for failure," said Jay Carver, the trustee who ran CSOSA from its 1997 inception until August 2000. "Parole supervision was a joke, and the inmates knew that."

Halfway houses for Lorton inmates were reopened in 1998. Carver had extraordinary success in gaining congressional funding, allowing more parole and probation officers to be hired. Case loads dropped from between 180 and 200 per officer to 50 or 60. A new system of quick, short incarcerations for minor offenses helped reinforce the message that parole officers were watching more closely.

"They have to be able to distinguish between people who aren't learning, and the hammer has to come down, and the people who are just having bumps on the road to recovery," said Eric Lotke, director of the Prisoners' Legal Services Project. "That's important, because it helps people who are trying to make it have a better shot at succeeding."

Meanwhile, more grass-roots programs popped up.

Sullivan's organization, CURE, began publishing a 308-page manual for newly released inmates. It's a detailed reference book listing "the first six things you must do after getting out" (getting a birth certificate is tops, after seeing your parole officer) and other information on getting new clothes, a job and a place to live.

In Southeast, a Lutheran Church ministry opened the Anacostia Men's Employment Network (AMEN) in 1997. Offered near Hope Village, the city's largest halfway house, the program began with three-week sessions in job placement. Program director Jeff Lea, a former personnel director in the hotel industry, said 60 former inmates have gotten jobs after completing the course, a placement rate of about 75 percent.

Chester Hart did 12 years for a variety of drug and robbery charges. He's on parole for another 40 years. But he's been out for 14 months, works at AMEN as a job counselor and hasn't had a single parole violation. He says he's out to stay.

"There is very little in the way of services that is waiting for you when you walk out of prison," he said. "So you've got to have a program like this to help you get settled, to get some momentum going."

A Sharp Turnaround

All of the former inmates interviewed for this story said they had resolved while in prison that they would change once they got out. Hart had been in and out of prisons for more than 20 years. He was sick of it.

Gantt converted to Christianity while incarcerated and got involved with a group called Concerned Fathers, which encourages inmates to stay involved in their children's lives.

After Gantt's family finally picked him up on Jan. 8, 1998, he went straight home. He went to church the next day. On the following Monday morning, the Alliance for Concerned Men—sponsors of the father's program in prison—offered him a $5 an hour job cleaning up its offices.

He took it. He's been building his future since then, working to keep his focus on the days ahead, not the life left behind. His turnaround has been so sharp, and he is so articulate, that he has a budding career as a motivational speaker.

"At any time, I'm just 24 hours from being back in prison," he said, referring to what could happen if he violates his parole. "But I'm not going to do anything like that. The old ways don't even interest me anymore. There are stresses—bumping into old friends who say I'm a fake, things like that—but I stay out of all that negativity. I've got my job going, my sons, my church. I'm out of that life."

*"The result [of parole] is that very few
[convicts] come close to serving . . . the
maximum to which they were sentenced."*

Parole and Probation Have Not Succeeded as Alternatives

Joseph M. Bessette

In the following viewpoint, Joseph M. Bessette argues that
parole and probation have not succeeded as alternatives to
imprisonment. He claims that courts and parole boards are
too lenient toward offenders, allowing even those who commit violent crimes such as rape and murder to serve fractions
of their sentences. Such "lax criminal codes" have frequently
allowed violent repeat offenders to be released into society. If
parole boards and the criminal justice system continue to be
too lenient, Bessette insists, these alternatives to imprisonment should be restricted or abolished. Bessette is a government and ethics professor at Claremont McKenna College.

As you read, consider the following questions:

1. How does the author support his claim that offenders
   serve out fractions of their sentences?
2. According to Bessette, why is the prison system not as
   expensive as widely perceived?
3. How does Bessette support his claim that crime rates
   rose during increased use of parole and probation?

Excerpted from "In Pursuit of Criminal Justice," by Joseph M. Bessette, *The Public
Interest*, October 15, 1997. Copyright © 1997 by National Affairs, Inc. Reprinted
with permission from the author and *The Public Interest*, no. 129, Fall 1997, pp. 61–72.

Despite evidence suggesting that much of American public policy closely—perhaps too closely—mirrors public desires (for example, Social Security, Medicare, and the federal college-loan program), this is hardly the case in how we punish violent criminals. Policy makers and criminal justice practitioners set punishment levels well below what the public considers appropriate. Indeed, our punishment practices reflect a pronounced disconnect between reasonable public opinion, on the one hand, and actual government policy, on the other. . . .

According to the National Punishment Survey conducted by the Population and Society Research Center at Bowling Green State University in 1987, the public recommends prison sentences for a variety of violent and other serious crimes approximately three times longer than offenders actually serve. And, according to U.S. Department of Justice data on actual time served by those leaving state prisons, half the murderers serve seven years or less, half the rapists serve less than four years, half the robbers serve two years and three months or less, half of those convicted of felony assault (often called aggravated assault) serve one year and four months or less, and half the drug traffickers serve one year and two months or less. Altogether, half of the 54,000 violent offenders who were released from prisons in 36 states in 1992 served two years or less behind bars. These data include many offenders with prior records and many convicted of multiple offenses at one time.

Even these figures fail to capture the full picture, for large numbers of those convicted of felonies receive sentences of straight probation (a period of supervision in the community) rather than incarceration. In 1994, state courts throughout the nation sentenced 29 percent of convicted felons to probation with no incarceration—a total of 253,000 offenders, including 2,400 rapists, 5,500 robbers, over 16,000 persons convicted of aggravated assault, and 48,000 drug traffickers. It is hardly conceivable that the American people agree with the granting of straight probation to so many convicted felons and violent offenders.

Why does our criminal justice system mete out so much less punishment than what the public wants? First, in many cases, state criminal codes are unusually, perhaps even inexplicably, lenient. For example, when in 1978 Minnesota pioneered the use of a sentencing-guidelines grid to rationalize sentencing for convicted felons, it stipulated that a rapist with no prior record serve just two years and five months in prison for his crime (a sentence of 43 months, minus a one-third good-time reduction). Similarly, in California, the presumptive sentence for rape between 1976 and 1994 was six years in state prison (which could drop to three years due to mitigating circumstances or increase to eight years with aggravating circumstances). The formal sentence was subject to various sentence-reduction credits, also stipulated in the penal code, that amounted to 50 percent for most of this period. Thus, until the California state legislature increased the potential punishment for the most serious rapes to an indeterminate 25 years to life in 1994, official state policy called for a mere three years behind bars for most rapes.

This short statutory punishment, together with strict limits on consecutive sentencing, partly explains why even serial rapists in California often serve unconscionably short prison terms for their crimes. Consider Christopher Evans Hubbart who terrorized young women in the suburbs east of Los Angeles in the 1970s and 1980s. Hubbart, whose modus operandi was to surprise women living alone by breaking into their homes in the early morning hours, was convicted in 1972 for raping 14 women. He served six years in state prison. On the very day of his release, he raped again. And, avoiding apprehension, he raped at least nine more women during the next two years. For these 10 new rapes, after being convicted in 1982, he served an additional eight years in prison.

Shortly after this second release, in 1990, Hubbart abducted another woman; this time he was sentenced to five years in prison. Denied early release several times because he failed psychiatric examinations, Hubbart would have been freed unconditionally in 1995 at the age of 45 had California not passed a new law that allowed sexual predators to be sent to a state mental hospital for an additional two years if it could be shown in civil court that the offender was still a danger to the community. For his 24 rape convictions (and he was suspected by authorities of many more), Hubbart served a total of 14 years behind bars, an average of seven months per rape. . . .

Discretion Too Far

Another reason why punishments often fall short of public expectations is judicial leniency. Well-publicized reductions in judicial discretion in recent decades, brought about by sentencing guidelines and mandatory minimum-sentencing laws in the federal system and some states, have done little to change this. In the majority of criminal convictions throughout the country, judges retain extraordinary power to choose probation or prison, to determine the length of prison sentences, to throw out collateral convictions, and to impose concurrent or consecutive sentences for the offenders with multiple convictions. Sometimes that discretion is exercised in ways that completely defy reasonable public judgments about just policy.

This was well demonstrated in a 1982 nationally publicized case when Ron Ebens and his stepson Michael Nitz, both unemployed auto workers, beat Chinese American Vincent Chin to death after an argument at a Detroit area bar. (The assault was precipitated by the offenders' belief that Chin was Japanese and thus shared responsibility for the downturn in the American auto industry.) For this crime, in which the offenders waited for Chin outside the bar, and one held him down while the other beat him to death with a baseball bat, the Wayne County judge sentenced the killers to probation and a $3,700 fine.

Early paroles also help explain our system's lenience. Sentences that sound tough when they are handed down can result in actual time in prison well under the stipulated maximum. Indeed, in most states, parole boards retain broad authority to release offenders once they are eligible under state law. The result is that very few come close to serving anything like the maximum to which they were sentenced. Nationally, the typical prison inmate serves only slightly more than one-third of his maximum sentence. Even violent offenders serve well under half of their maximum. The fact that a few famous prison inmates such as Charles Manson and Sirhan Sirhan are continually denied parole obscures the broader reality: Nearly all those eligible for parole eventually receive it. . . .

The Invisible Hand of Leniency

Some argue that the public, despite its dissatisfaction with current punishment levels, is unwilling to pay the costs of increased punishment. Yet this hardly seems tenable. Only 1.1 percent of all government spending in this country is devoted to building and operating all of our prisons and to running all of our *probation* and parole programs. Even doubling or tripling this amount would not raise corrections spending to more than a tiny fraction of all government spending. It is true, of course, that corrections costs are a higher fraction of state-government spending, since state governments finance most of the nation's prisons. But even here the proportion is in the range of 4 percent to 5 percent, far less than what is spent on education and social welfare. With the average American contributing about 30 cents per day to cover the nation's entire correctional budget (including probation and parole), insufficient resources can hardly explain why half the rapists are serving less than four years or why 253,000 convicted felons each year receive a straight probation sentence.

What, then, accounts for the divergence between public opinion and public policy? In important respects punishment policy in the United States is the accumulation of millions of individual decisions each year: decisions about whether to arrest an individual; whether to prosecute him; whether to drop some charges or offer a break on the sentence through a plea bargain; whether to send the convicted offender to probation or prison; whether to imprison those who violate probation; how long to make prison sentences; whether to make sentences for multiple crimes concurrent or consecutive; whether to rescind good-time credits for misbehavior in prison; whether to parole from prison eligible offenders; and whether to return to prison those who violate the conditions of release. While we have excellent statistical information on the aggregate results of these decisions, the public is still essentially ignorant, in all but a few high-publicity cases each year, of the specific punishment decisions made in their community. . . .

The other factor is the set of ideas about punishment that govern the thinking of criminal justice decision makers. Those who work within the system do not share the broader public's judgments about punishment, and they are, for the most part, free from public scrutiny. Many hold views closer to those of Ramsey Clark or Karl Menninger than to those of the average citizen. Clark, just a few years after serving as U.S. Attorney General for Lyndon Johnson, wrote that "punishment as an end in itself is itself a crime in our times." Clark endorsed the views of psychiatrist Karl Menninger, who maintained that punishment is "our crime against criminals—and, incidentally, our crime against ourselves. We must renounce the philosophy of punishment, the obsolete, vengeful penal attitude."

For the Ultimate Crime

For the ultimate crime of murder, society must have the courage to take a stand, denounce the act as abhorrent, vow not to tolerate it and follow through with a tough sentence. The murderer has proven his or her lack of respect for human life and deserves to be segregated from society, not only as a penalty but for the safety of the rest of us.

Jean Lewis, *Corrections Today*, December 1997.

During the 1950s and 1960s, states made rehabilitation rather than punishment the central principle of penal policy. Probation became more widely used, along with indeterminate sentences and liberal release practices. Parole boards began assessing the prisoner's fitness for release, not whether he had suffered a punishment commensurate with his crime. The predominance of this ideology of rehabilitation explains why the nation's prison population did not increase between 1960 and 1975 (and actually declined between 1960 and 1968) at the very time when serious crimes reported to the police more than tripled (from 3.4 million to 11.3 million), when the violent crimes of murder, rape, robbery, and aggravated assault increased three and one-half times (from 288,000 to one million), and when arrests for serious crimes increased two and one-half times.

Despite the fact that the rehabilitation approach has fallen out of public favor—and one now rarely hears it publicly defended as the basis for sentencing adult offenders—approximately three-fourths of the states still retain the essential mechanisms of the rehabilitation ideology: the indeterminate sentence and discretionary parole-board release. . . .

Justice for All

Although complete freedom from crime is an unrealistic goal, a substantial reduction in serious and violent crime is not. The most constructive way to move toward that reduction, building upon recent encouraging trends, is to embrace standards of just punishment that approximate reasonable public judgments. Here the challenge lies primarily with state legislatures, for they are the original source of our punishment policies and practices. If the state penal codes themselves prescribe punishments well below public standards, then they should be rewritten and brought into line with public opinion. If judges are too lenient in how they exercise their sentencing discretion, then the legislature can establish presumptive sentences or mandatory minimums for serious offenders or recidivists. If parole boards are too generous in granting releases from prison, then parole can be restricted or even abolished (as about one-fourth of the states have done during the past two decades). . . .

By bringing punishment more in line with public judgments about what offenders deserve, we will incapacitate recidivists, more effectively deter would-be criminals, and enhance public confidence in our governing institutions. Finally, by reaffirming and enforcing the precepts of the moral order, we can provide essential institutional support for the good efforts of parents, preachers, and teachers to fashion a law-abiding community.

"In prison, [a drug offender] has little chance of being given the treatment—the tools—to beat the addiction."

Drug Treatment Can Succeed as an Alternative

Cristina Everett

Various states have begun sentencing nonviolent drug offenders to drug treatment instead of prison in order to decrease prison overcrowding and reduce drug-related crime. For example in California, Proposition 36, which was passed by voters in the November 2000 election, gives drug offenders the option to attend drug treatment instead of going to jail or prison. In the following viewpoint, Cristina Everett argues in favor of Proposition 36. She asserts that prisons do not offer drug offenders the tools to fight their addictions. Drug offenders, she insists, should be sentenced to work on breaking their addictions instead of "biding time until the next fix." Everett, a California resident, actively campaigned for Proposition 36.

As you read, consider the following questions:
1. How does Everett support her claim that drug treatment is less expensive than incarceration?
2. According to the author, who opposes Proposition 36, and why?
3. According to Everett, how is the power of judges preserved by Proposition 36?

Excerpted from "Treatment, Not Prison, Best Solution for Drug Offenders," by Cristina Everett, *Daily Bruin*, October 19, 2000. Reprinted with permission from the *Daily Bruin*.

Consider this: a person is arrested for simple drug possession. Although no other crime has been committed, this person is sentenced to a jail term. Perhaps this person has an addiction problem. In prison, this person has little chance of being given the treatment—the tools—to beat the addiction and return to society as a contributing member. They are released still addicted, with a criminal record, and unable to reintegrate into society. They are set up to fail.

For Drug Addicts, Not Criminals

Proposition 36 is about treatment as opposed to incarceration for the type of drug offender who is most likely to benefit from treatment. Proposition 36 does not apply to anyone who has committed a concurrent criminal act or has a violent history. Proposition 36 aims to catch drug addicts before they get into the cycle of resorting to harmful and dangerous activity to support their habit. This is why it is called the Substance Abuse and Crime Prevention Act.

Who supports Proposition 36? The list of endorsers is long and diverse. A sampling: California Association of Alcoholism and Drug Abuse Counselors, California Psychiatric Association, California Women's Commission, Progressive Jewish Alliance, Republican Liberty Caucus, Rainbow Caucus of the California Democratic Party, Dolores Huerta of United Farm Workers/AFL-CIO, Willie L. Brown—Mayor of San Francisco, and the California Public Defenders Association.

These individuals and groups know that drug addicts must be treated for the benefit of themselves and society rather than warehoused in prison at a cost to taxpayers of upwards of $25,000 per year.

That brings us to the simple economic issue. In approximate numbers, reputable treatment would cost the state $5,000 a year per case. As stated earlier, incarceration runs the state about $25,000 a year per case. In the state of California, there are approximately 19,700 people in prison for simple drug possession offenses.

Fewer prisoners means no need for new prisons. More prison space will be reserved for the truly violent criminals who pose a threat to society. Fewer prisons and prisoners is why the non-partisan state Legislative Analyst believes that Proposition 36 will save California taxpayers $1.5 billion.

Not for Drug Decriminalization

Who opposes Proposition 36? The very groups that would benefit from more prisoners. A few examples are the California Probation, Parole and Correctional Association, California Bail Agents and the California Correctional Peace Officers Association. The CCPOA is one of the largest lobby groups in California. They have an obvious vested interest in the growth of the prison population and the development of new prison facilities.

What do our opponents say? Those in opposition to Proposition 36 claim that the proposition seeks to decriminalize drugs. Not true. To be diverted under Proposition 36 means offenders are convicted of a felony and placed on probation, like many other criminals. Proposition 36 simply

---

Reaching Drug Offenders

I want to be very clear about the offenses that Prop 36 reaches. We're only talking here about drug possession or being under the influence. But people who are dealing drugs, people who commit another crime at the same time as the drug possession, or people who have a fairly recent history of any other serious or violent felonies are completely excluded. So we're not talking right now about people who have shown propensity to violence and who have not committed any other kind of crime, except for their drug addiction becoming evident through their being arrested in possession.

So these people can't be declared automatically to be generally a threat to society. Mostly we're talking about people who have a problem. And the question then becomes, "What do we do to deal with it?" Putting them in jail doesn't stop them from using drugs, that's for sure, and the recidivism rates are incredible. If you don't give somebody treatment when you've got the opportunity, you've got them in front of the court, you've got them under the control of the criminal justice system, and you don't give them any services, which is what we're doing now for probably 95 percent of drug offenders in California who don't get into drug court, you're just going to see them again. And then they will go down that cycle.

Dave Fratello, interviewed by Juan Williams, *Talk of the Nation*, August 3, 2000.

---

changes sentencing; instead of incarcerating addicts, their criminal sentence is treatment, plus any other sanctions deemed necessary by the court. Instead of biding time until the next fix while in jail, an offender can work toward changing a dangerous lifestyle.

Simply put: you don't put a fire out by yelling at or ignoring it; rather, you take quick action to douse the flames.

Opponents also argue that we already have a sufficient system in place with the drug courts. Yet while drug courts do offer alternatives to prison, currently they only serve about 2 percent of the population that could qualify for the program. Proposition 36 would extend the reach of the drug courts and give a much larger population access to effective treatment.

Furthermore, they say that Proposition 36 will render the drug court judges powerless. Again, not true. A judge will have the power to determine what treatment program would be most appropriate and would supervise the offender until the offender was sufficiently recovered. Offenders can be, at the discretion of a judge, sentenced to one to three years in state prison if they do not prove themselves amenable to treatment.

Finally, opponents claim that Proposition 36 opens the door for fly-by-night treatment providers including such things as "online" treatment programs. This is simply not true. Every treatment provider must be accredited by the state, and a judge has the final word on which treatment provider is the most effective for each individual offender.

The Tools to Fight Drug Addiction

Who am I that you should take my opinion to your local polling place? I am someone quite like yourself. I am a UCLA graduate (1990), a former public school educator, someone who read the admittedly technical language of Proposition 36 and came out for the side of effectiveness, fairness, and what would be the most safe and healthy choice for our community.

Why should you care? Because you . . . will make choices that continue to benefit future generations of Californians. Because you are, or will soon be, a taxpayer who cares how your hard earned money is managed. Because if you have ever . . . made a mistake, you would be grateful for the tools and the time to go back and . . . fix the mistake.

A "yes" vote on Proposition 36 will give medical professionals the necessary tools to help people suffering from drug addiction. Such treatment will help addicts return to society as healthier, more stable and more productive individuals.

"Not all drug offenders are amenable to treatment. . . . The shock of prison may be a better therapeutic alternative."

Drug Offenders Should Be Imprisoned

Charles L. Hobson

Many jurisdictions are experimenting with sentencing non-violent drug offenders to treatment instead of prison. Passed by California voters in the November 2000 election, Proposition 36 gives a first-time drug offender the option to go to treatment instead of prison. If the drug offender violates probation three times, he or she will be imprisoned. In the following viewpoint, Charles L. Hobson asserts that this initiative is flawed because imprisonment is necessary to treat most drug offenders. Hobson argues that the threat of imprisonment provides an incentive for drug users to break their addictions. He adds that many drug offenders are dangerous, and failing to imprison them puts public safety at risk. Hobson is the attorney for the Criminal Justice Legal Foundation, a nonprofit public interest law organization.

As you read, consider the following questions:

1. How does the author support his claim that Proposition 36 is "based upon faulty research"?
2. In Hobson's view, how can placing drug offenders in drug treatment, not prison, threaten public safety?
3. According to Hobson, how can increasing the numbers of drug treatment centers threaten public safety?

Excerpted from "An Analysis of Proposition 36, The Drug Treatment Diversion Initiative," by Charles L. Hobson, released by the Criminal Legal Justice Foundation, October 27, 2000. Reprinted with permission from CLJF. Article available at www.noonprop36.com.

The Drug Treatment Diversion Initiative ("Initiative") is yet another attempt to solve the drug problem through a single comprehensive plan. It replaces the current system of treating drug offenders, where offenders are diverted from punishment to drug treatment at the discretion of district attorneys and judges, with a mandatory system that applies to almost all low-level drug offenders without regard to their amenability to treatment or potential danger to society.

Although diversion of low-level offenders to drug treatment programs can be beneficial, this virtual decriminalization of drug possession and personal use does more harm than good. This proposition is based upon a flawed interpretation of prior drug treatment efforts. It will waste resources on undeserving participants at the expense of public safety and more deserving individuals with drug problems. The many serious problems with this proposal outweigh any incidental advantages.

Based upon Faulty Research

The Initiative places great emphasis on the ability of drug treatment programs to prevent future drug use and other criminal behavior. Section 2, subdivision (a) states that nonviolent, drug dependent criminal offenders who receive drug treatment are much less likely to abuse drugs and commit future crimes. . . . Subdivision (c) of Section 2 cites a 1996 Arizona drug treatment initiative as support for this proposition.

While drug treatment programs are useful in reducing some crime and suffering, the Initiative's claims are extravagant in light of current experience. As there has not been enough time to make an appropriately rigorous analysis of this program, Arizona's experience cannot justify the Initiative. The Arizona program shows that in the first year of its mandatory treatment program, only 35.5% of the offenders completed their treatment program. Of those 35.5% only 61.1% completed their treatment program successfully, a rate of 21.6%. Any indicators of success, such as the seemingly high rate of negative drug tests, thus must be placed in the context of the small number of successful completions and the preliminary state of the data.

Drug treatment programs can help reduce drugs and crime.

Specialty drug courts have proven useful in lowering the recidivism and drug use of drug offenders. This is not, however, a miracle cure for drugs and crime. Drug addiction and the associated criminality are both very difficult habits to break. Thus while some well-designed, carefully monitored programs will help lessen the drug-crime cycle, too many poorly implemented programs have little effect on reducing addiction or recidivism. For example, in a Maricopa County, Arizona drug court program that occurred before the Arizona initiative, offenders in the drug program had slightly more new arrests than those in the control group that did not participate in the program. Poorly supervised programs can even be fronts for criminal activity. Therefore, strong oversight is essential to any successful treatment program. Unfortunately, the Initiative weakens the monitoring systems for drug treatment. Wasted resources and broken promises are almost inevitable.

Promising more than it can deliver has been the bane of the drug treatment movement. Reality brings with it inevitable public disappointment, which has in turn undercut support for drug treatment programs. The Initiative poses a similar threat to drug treatment, by making promises that cannot be kept it may result in harming the cause it seeks to help.

Diversion Threatens Public Safety and Wastes Resources

The most important difference between the Initiative and current practice is one of the Initiative's greatest flaws, mandatory diversion. The current system allows for diversion but vests considerable discretion in the court to determine whether the accused should be diverted. Under California law, the district attorney must first find that the accused is eligible for diversion. The trial court then holds a hearing to determine whether diversion would benefit the accused. Diversion is granted only if this standard is satisfied at the trial court's discretion.

The Initiative replaces this carefully guided discretion with a system of mandatory diversion with few minimal eligibility requirements. This is a serious mistake. Although some may be helped by diversion, others should not be placed in the program. Many drug offenders pose a real threat to public safety. Thus, a spousal abuser whose victim will not file a complaint should not be given the benefit of diversion; jailing him for a minor drug crime may be the best chance to break the abuse cycle. The Initiative's protections are not enough. Although the Initiative bars from diversion some who have been previously convicted of serious or violent felonies, this does not extend to out-of-state convictions. Therefore someone with out-of-state convictions for rape or drug-related murders must be diverted without regard to the obvious threat to public safety of keeping such a person on the streets. . . .

A Criminal Threat

[Proposition 36] relies almost exclusively on treatment and thus fails to protect citizens from the very real criminal and public health threat posed by the illegal drug trade. . . .

Because [drug offenders] are addicted to a dangerous and illegal substance, they often rely on a criminal market to satisfy their habits, and bring that dangerous market to the poor and vulnerable neighborhoods where they usually live.

Sacramento Bee, October 14, 2000.

This inflexibility is wasteful as well as dangerous. Not all drug offenders are amenable to treatment. Yet the Initiative would place all offenders in treatment, even if the shock of prison may be a better therapeutic alternative, or more appropriate punishment. Placing people in therapy they do not deserve wastes resources. Even though the Initiative may increase funding for drug treatment, it will also substantially increase the demand for treatment. Resources are never infinite. Diverting scarce treatment resources to undeserving convicts will inevitably deprive some deserving offenders of necessary treatments.

Deciding who should be eligible for treatment is the single most difficult problem facing any drug treatment program. This is how a program preserves public safety while diverting scarce resources to those who can best utilize them. The Initiative, by opening the treatment center's doors to almost everyone, hopelessly compromises this principle, thus threatening the integrity of this state's drug treatment programs.

Jail Time Is Necessary

The Initiative makes it extraordinarily difficult to imprison someone for drug possession or use. An offender under the program has to violate probation three times before it is automatically revoked. Before that, the State must prove that he is a danger to society for the first violation, or dangerous or not amenable to treatment after the second violation.

Authorities agree that the threat or coercion of jail time is a necessary part of any successful treatment program for drug offenders. While an occasional relapse may not warrant immediate imprisonment, the threat of real punishment is too remote under this plan. This can only harm drug offenders by undermining this necessary incentive to rehabilitate....

A Danger to Neighborhoods

In *Bay Area Addiction Research v. City of Antioch* the Ninth Circuit Court of Appeals held that the Americans with Disabilities Act is very likely to prevent cities from using their zoning power to keep drug rehabilitation centers out of residential areas. Since the Initiative will significantly increase demand for treatment, it is likely that many more centers will be built. Many of these new centers will be in residential areas, given the relatively low rents of residential space in comparison to commercial areas. Since the Initiative makes only minimal provisions for excluding dangerous offenders, the threat to neighborhoods is much higher than under current law. If the Initiative passes, many Californians may find new neighbors, such as a methadone clinic or a methamphetamine treatment center full of insufficiently screened drug offenders. This can only compound the danger posed by the Initiative's rigid inclusion.

A Poisoned Chalice

Although well-intended, the Initiative is a poisoned chalice for both the drug treatment movement and Californians. It uses faulty research to over expand a somewhat useful program for treating some low-level offenders into a therapeutic leviathan. Its mandatory inclusion is both dangerous and wasteful. If there are deserving individuals who are currently not receiving diversion, it is more likely due to a lack of resources than any deficiencies in California law. Drug addicts, public safety, and fiscal sensibilities, would all be better served by simply allocating more resources into current programs and passing legislation allowing searches as a condition to diversion. The dramatic changes to current law are at best unnecessary, and most likely counterproductive. A public reaction to the Initiative's unfulfilled promises and public danger is almost inevitable. This reaction will almost certainly compound the harm done to drug rehabilitation by this misguided initiative.

"*Many judges and sentencing experts argue that creative sentences can serve both justice and the community.*"

Creative Sentencing Can Provide Effective Alternatives

David Mulholland

Creative sentencing refers to punishments tailored to fit the crime and rehabilitate the offender. For example, an adolescent convicted of vandalism was sentenced by a teen court to guard and clean the wall he vandalized. Another court, attempting to keep drunk driving offenders sober, gave them the option to take home alcohol-monitoring devices instead of posting bail. In the following viewpoint, David Mulholland suggests that creative sentencing can be more effective than imprisonment for many offenders. He asserts that its flexibility gives punishments more meaning by allowing judges to rehabilitate offenders and sentence them to serve the community. Moreover, creative sentencing can divert minor offenders from prisons and reduce prison overcrowding. Mulholland is a staff reporter at the *Wall Street Journal*.

As you read, consider the following questions:

1. In Mulholland's view, for what reasons do judges seek out creative sentencing?
2. According to the author, why do opponents argue against creative sentencing?
3. According to Mulholland, what incentives of sentence reduction did Judge Joe B. Brown offer to many young offenders?

When a young nonviolent offender was sentenced recently in Memphis, Tenn., Judge Joe B. Brown didn't send her to jail. He ordered her to write a 3,000-word essay about "Crooklyn," a Spike Lee film about urban family life, relating the film to her life and explaining why she should get probation.

Though Spike Lee films usually aren't involved, alternative sentencing programs that give judges options other than prison or parole are on the rise. Ten years ago there were about 20 programs nationwide; now there are more than 300, says Mark Mauer, assistant director of the Sentencing Project, a Washington, D.C., group that promotes the use of sentencing experts for most nonviolent crimes. Sentencing experts—usually lawyers or social workers—put together sentencing packages appropriate to the criminal and the crime with a view toward rehabilitation.

Serving Justice

Tight budgets and overcrowded prisons are two reasons judges want to find new ways to punish criminals who aren't considered to be a threat to society. In some cases, alternatives such as community service are ordered in addition to other penalties, including fines and jail. For example, skater Tonya Harding is serving food to seniors for her community service for her part in the attack on Olympic rival Nancy Kerrigan.

But critics say justice is poorly served by letting some criminals stay out of jail. One problem with alternative sentencing is determining who is a good candidate, says Paul McNulty, co-founder of the First Freedom Coalition, a nonprofit group that advocates changing the criminal justice system. "Most alternatives involve release," he says. "Someone convicted on a drugs charge without a gun could still be dangerous to society."

But many judges and sentencing experts argue that creative sentences can serve both justice and the community. As part of his sentence for molesting two students, a 66-year-old Houston music instructor was forced to give up his $12,000 piano and post a sign on his front door warning children to stay away. State District Judge Ted Poe, known for unusual sentencings, also barred the teacher from buying another piano, and even from playing one until the end of his 20-year probation. The judge noted that the instructor had stolen the two girls' desire to play.

In Portland, Maine, a Bowdoin College graduate convicted of smuggling several thousand pounds of marijuana was sentenced to set up and run an AIDS hospice. The logic? The city needed the hospice, and the smuggler had the organizational and business savvy to make it work.

Edmonton, Canada, is cracking down on prostitution, making 1994 the "Year of the John." As part of the sentence for clients picked up in prostitution busts, Judge Sharon Vandeveen informs their wives. Dr. Barbara Romanowski, director of Sexually Transmitted Disease Services in Edmonton, has proposed that the clients pick up used condoms in skin-trade areas as part of community service penalties.

In Isanti County, Minn., Judge James Dehn, who teaches creative sentencing, gives people accused of drunken driving a choice of $1,500 bail or breathing into a home alcohol-monitoring device three times a day until the trial. The machine is hooked up to the telephone. A computer at the police station calls the machine and can determine if the accused has been drinking. If so, or if the accused didn't breathe into the device, he or she goes to jail. Most people choose the device, which they rent for $77 a week; no one has failed yet.

Traditional, Creative, and Meaningful

In Memphis, Judge Brown's sentences combine traditional and creative elements. The municipal judge argues that locking people up for longer and longer periods isn't working. He says the people he sentences typically are young drug users with no employment skills and long juvenile records.

Judge Brown says that, depending on the crime, his usual sentence for such offenders is two years in prison and five years of probation, with the incentive of sentence reduction if the offender passes the GED—a test of high school equivalency—and successfully completes a drug rehabilitation program.

Judge Brown also sends people to counseling; of some he requires reading assignments and book reports, which he grades. Often he adds a punishment that is "particularly meaningful to the defendant," he says. One example is taking burglary victims to the thief's home and inviting them to take whatever they want.

Restorative Justice

[One] alternative-sentencing program is part of a strategy aimed at engaging a criminal's conscience. The effort unites judges, attorneys, prosecutors and police with one objective: help restore the victims of crime by getting offenders to take personal responsibility for their acts. Called "restorative justice," the approach draws on traditional ideas about guilt, responsibility and restitution—ideas whose origin is the Bible. In both the Old and New Testaments, crime is considered an offense not primarily against society, but against individuals. And restoring the victims of crime always involves making amends.

Restorative justice, then, is justice that is up close and personal. It involves face-to-face meetings between victim and offender. It means striking agreements on restitution by tapping into paychecks or ordering community service.

Joe Loconte, *USA Today*, April 13, 1998.

He even sentenced one check forger to watch a caged gorilla for an hour. "I wanted him to get the idea of why this gorilla was looking so bored, and it came to him. 'It's because the gorilla's in jail and doing nothing,'" says Judge Brown.

Serving the Community

Alternative sentences are also used in courts run by teenagers, with a real judge presiding, that have sprung up across the country. Usually the adolescent jurors only decide the duration of a teenage defendant's community service. But in a teen court started April 1993 at Munroe High School in Northridge, a suburb of Los Angeles, and more recently at Wilson High School in Los Angeles, the jurors decide guilt and provide Judge Jaime Corral with a sentencing suggestion. In one case a graffiti "tagger"—someone who puts gang or personal logos on walls—was sentenced to six months of guarding the wall he vandalized. If anyone marked the wall, he had to clean it.

Recidivism at Munroe and Wilson has been much lower than in schools without the courts, according to Judge Corral. Fewer than 5% of the people sentenced with wrongdoing have broken the law again.

By far the most common community service is cleaning roads, parks and buildings with city agencies. Since 1983, "special service crews" have performed community service by doing work for Caltrans, California's highway maintenance department. Between 8,000 and 10,000 people a year serve out their sentences by painting over graffiti, cleaning up trash and pulling weeds. The crews are monitored to ensure the prescribed hours of community service are performed. Spokesman Jim Drago says the practice has saved the agency about $80 million [from 1984 to 1994].

| "*[Creative sentences] give voice to a community's fury and moral disgust, but they solve little in the long run.*"

Creative Sentencing May Not Provide Effective Alternatives

Jeffrey Abramson

Creative sentencing is an effort to make punishment more meaningful by designing a sentence to rehabilitate an offender and serve the community. However, some creative sentences have been controversial. For instance, a mother convicted of child abuse agreed to be implanted with a Norplant contraceptive as part of her probation. In California, parole has been granted to convicted child molesters who agreed to undergo "chemical castration" to suppress their libidos. In the following viewpoint, Jeffrey Abramson asserts that creative sentencing may not provide effective alternatives to prison. He contends that it expresses the rage and frustration a community feels toward an offender, which is a "haphazard" approach to punishment. Therefore, he claims that creative sentences often have little or no rehabilitative value. Abramson is a professor of politics and legal studies at Brandeis University.

As you read, consider the following questions:
1. What "provocative" examples of "smart sentencing" does the author cite?
2. What example does Abramson give to support his claim that "Scarlet Letter" punishments are in fashion?
3. Why does Abramson believe creative punishments will not deter crime?

Reprinted from "Are Courts Getting Too Creative?" by Jeffrey Abramson, *The New York Times*, March 11, 1999. Reprinted with permission from *The New York Times*.

Buried on the sports pages in March 1999 was a very modern tale of crime and punishment, one involving AIDS, football players and solicitation of prostitution.

On the eve of 1999's Super Bowl in Miami, Eugene Robinson, a safety for the Atlanta Falcons, was arrested on a charge of soliciting sex from an undercover police officer. Robinson could have been convicted and sentenced to up to 60 days in jail. Instead, he agreed to enter an alternative program where his "punishment" would be to undergo an H.I.V. test and to enroll in an AIDS education course.

Both sides got what they wanted: Robinson avoided having a criminal record, and Miami-Dade County succeeded in getting its public health message across.

Since few advocate sending someone who has committed an act as minor as soliciting prostitution to a crowded jail, Robinson's case was a good one to try out alternative forms of justice. The prosecutors may even be hoping that the prospect of being forced to undergo H.I.V. testing will do more to deter men from soliciting prostitutes than the increasingly idle threat of jail time.

Smart Sentencing?

Other cities are experimenting with even more creative alternative penalties, but not all of them are so laudable. Many have revived old-style public shaming by posting the names of people convicted of soliciting prostitutes on billboards or announcing them on local cable television.

Such alternative sentences have typically been imposed as a condition of probation or as part of a plea bargain or pretrial diversion program where the defendant voluntarily agrees to sentencing conditions that the judge might not otherwise be authorized to impose. As a result, trial judges today enjoy surprisingly broad discretion, even in this era of mandatory sentencing laws, to tailor the punishment to fit the crime.

This movement, known as smart sentencing, has created some rulings that are extremely provocative. For instance, a judge in Memphis has allowed victims of theft to take items from the burglar's home. In other cases, convicted felons must accept great invasions of privacy to become eligible for parole or probation. For example, a California law grants parole for repeat child molesters only if they undergo "chemical castration," which lowers testosterone levels.

But this style of sentencing is growing in popularity because it allows communities to express moral outrage in an immediate, dramatic and public fashion. It also taps into people's frustration with conduct that diminishes their quality of life.

Scarlet Letter Punishments

"Scarlet Letter" punishments in particular seem to be on the rise. In New York in 1998, a trial judge sentenced a slumlord to sleep in one of her own rental units to insure the building would be adequately heated through the winter. In California, a judge required a burglar to wear a T-shirt proclaiming, "I am a felon on probation for theft." In 1995, a judge on Long Island ordered a man convicted of drunken driving to display a license plate branding him as a convicted felon. (An appeals court overturned the sentence.)

Not for a Civil Country

Not everyone agrees with [creative] sentencing. Nationwide, attorneys with the American Civil Liberties Union have spoken out, often calling it cruel and unusual.

"If we go back to allowing judges to create their own punishments, we'll have fanatical judges running amok with citizens' rights," said Diana Philip, ACLU regional director of northern Texas. "I hope we're civil enough as a country not to let that happen."

Nicole Koch, *Dallas Morning News*, June 18, 1998.

In Port St. Lucie, Fla., a judge ordered a woman to place an advertisement in her local paper confessing that she had bought drugs in front of her children. In Houston, a man convicted of domestic violence in 1997 had to stand on the steps of City Hall and apologize for hitting his estranged wife. In Pittsfield, Ill., a 62-year-old farmer convicted of assault was granted probation—but only if he would agree to display a sign on his farm warning passers-by that "A Violent Felon Lives Here." Judges in Arkansas and Wisconsin have required convicted shoplifters to stand in front of stores and carry signs admitting their crimes.

Some judges have also included a kind of aversion therapy in their choices of punishment. In Colorado, a judge has recently been sentencing young people who have been arrested for playing music too loudly to sit in a club and listen to court-ordered music—like the "Barney" theme song. In Maryland, a man who was convicted of selling false insurance policies to horse trainers was made to clean out the stables of Baltimore's mounted police unit.

Haphazard and Whimsical

Ideally, smart sentencing could free judges from one-size-fits-all punishment. But the problem with these experimental sentences is that they seem haphazard, even whimsical at times. They give voice to a community's fury and moral disgust, but they solve little in the long run.

It is difficult to believe, for instance, that the urge to beat a spouse would be easily checked by humiliating the abuser in public. Psychologists have warned that this kind of punishment could backfire by fueling rage and resentment. Anthropologists have also found that many traditional cultures that practiced public shaming as punishment provided specific steps the accused could take to restore themselves into the community's grace. But advocates of smart sentencing have not yet managed to do this.

Creative sentencing can also be counterproductive when judges use community service like building affordable housing or working at a shelter for battered women as "punishment." For those who willingly work at these jobs, the idea that such valuable work is a fit form of criminal punishment must seem a rude insult.

The largest unanswered question about alternative sentencing is what limits we should place on judges. Do we really want them to be able to order felons on probation to attend church, as has happened in Kansas, in violation of the First Amendment? Convicted felons may have diminished expectations of privacy, but it still seems shocking that some judges have tried to compel convicted child abusers to have the contraceptive device Norplant implanted as a condition of probation.

Pushing Against the Limits

In Massachusetts, a convicted sex offender who has lived in the community for a year without incident has married, and the couple are expecting a child. But the terms of his parole prohibit him from having contact with any child under the age of 18, even his own. As sensible as most restrictions on sex offenders may be, this one pushes against the limits of punishment.

The Miami prosecutors may have been right in deciding more public good would be gained by sentencing Eugene Robinson to H.I.V. testing than to jail. But compare that with other alternative punishments that are pure gimmick: in Gastonia, N.C., a judge sentenced a man who rammed his truck into a car driven by an interracial couple to watch the movie "Mississippi Burning." Clearly, we need to put more thought into smart sentencing if we're going to separate the good aspects from the bad.

"Does it make sense to reject shaming—a strictly symbolic punishment—without giving it a fair try?"

Shame-Based Punishment Can Be an Effective Alternative

Amitai Etzioni

Shame-based punishments use the power of shame to punish offenders and deter crime. For instance, the pictures and names of known prostitutes and "johns" (their solicitors) have been broadcast on local television stations to discourage prostitution in a community. In the following viewpoint, Amitai Etzioni argues that modern shame-based punishment can be more effective than imprisonment. He contends that this approach can solve the major challenges facing the prison system, such as high maintenance costs and prison overcrowding. Unlike the shaming practices of colonial times, he adds, shame-based punishments today can be more humane and better suited for minor offenders than prison. Etzioni is a professor and director of the Center for Communitarian Policy Studies at the George Washington University.

As you read, consider the following questions:
1. In Etzioni's opinion, in what ways should "bad Samaritans" be punished?
2. What criticisms of shaming does Etzioni confront?
3. According to the author, how is shaming a "democratic" act?

Excerpted from "Back to the Pillory?" by Amitai Etzioni, *The American Scholar*, Summer 1999. Copyright © 1999 by Amitai Etzioni. Reprinted with permission from *The American Scholar*, vol. 68, no. 3.

Should young drug dealers, the first time they are caught peddling, be sent home with their heads shaved and without their pants instead of being jailed? When I cautiously floated this suggestion in a conversation over dinner with some liberal friends, they rolled their eyes and stared at me with dismay. I tried to explain that if the same youngsters are jailed, they are likely to be released as more hardened criminals than they were when they were arrested, that rehabilitation in prisons is practically unknown, and that young inmates are often abused. At that point, one of my friends asked if my next suggestion would be to mark offenders with scarlet letters. The others changed the subject.

The Merit of Shaming

A few weeks after this dinner conversation, a tragedy brought the merit of shaming back into public and scholarly discussion. I was a member of a panel of lawyers and academics who were asked by National Public Radio to discuss the rape and murder of a seven-year-old girl in a women's bathroom at a Las Vegas casino. We focused most of our attention not on the child's father, who had left his daughter roaming the casino at 3:30 A.M., or on Jeremy Strohmeyer, who had committed the crimes, but on a friend of the murderer named David Cash. After accompanying Strohmeyer to the bathroom, Cash had neither tried to stop the savaging of Sherrice Iverson nor informed the police afterward.

Among the members of our panel was Congressman Nicholas Lampson. Outraged by Cash's failure to intervene, Lampson had drafted a Good Samaritan bill that would impose severe punishments on those who fail to stop a sexual crime against a child when they could do so at little risk to themselves, or who do not report such offenses to public authorities. UCLA law professor Peter Aranella, another panel member, argued that these punishments were too severe and suggested that a shorter jail sentence would suffice. Elizabeth Semil, a member of the National Association of Criminal Defense Lawyers, was even more critical, commenting that "punitive legislation, criminal legislation, isn't the proper response." She also wondered "whether making it criminal to fail to act is good public policy. In other words, is it going to assist in solving the problem? And my response to that is: absolutely not.". . .

I suggested shaming. Instead of jailing future Cashes, the law should require that the names of bad Samaritans be posted on a Web site and in advertisements (paid for by the offenders) in key newspapers. Such postings would remove any remaining ambiguities about what society expects from people who can help others when there is no serious risk to their own well-being. And those with a weak conscience or a faltering civic sense would be nudged to do the right thing by fearing that their names would be added to the list of bad Samaritans, that their friends and families would chide them, that their neighbors would snicker.

While there are no statistics on the matter, it seems to me that judges, in an attempt to find a middle course between jailing offenders and allowing them to walk off scot-free, have tried shaming far more frequently of late than they did a decade or two ago. People convicted of driving under the influence of alcohol in Fort Bend County, Texas, have been sentenced to place "DUI" bumper stickers on their cars. A child molester in Port St. Lucie, Florida, was ordered by a judge to mark his property with a sign warning away children. The same judge ordered a woman convicted of purchasing drugs in front of her children to run a notice in the local newspaper detailing her offense. A Rhode Island man was ordered to publish the following four-by-six-inch notice, accompanied by his photograph: "I am Stephen Germershausen. I am 29 years old. . . . I was convicted of child molestation. . . . If you are a child molester, get professional help immediately, or you may find your picture and name in the paper." A Tennessee judge sentenced a convicted defendant to confess before a church congregation his crime of abetting the sale of a stolen vehicle. Syracuse puts embarrassing signs in front of buildings owned by slumlords; Des Moines publishes their names in newspapers.

Waves of Criticism

Far from being widely hailed as a more humane and just way of punishing offenders and deterring others, such instances of judicial shaming have raised waves of criticism. Nadine

Strossen, president of the American Civil Liberties Union, wrote, "I'm very skeptical when criminologists and sociologists say that the best way to rehabilitate someone is to isolate him and put some sort of scarlet letter on him. We need to integrate criminals back into our community." According to Mark Kappelhoff, legislative counsel at the ACLU, "Gratuitous humiliation of the individual serves no societal purpose at all . . . and there's been no research to suggest it's been effective in reducing crime.". . .

Law professor Erwin Cherminsky observed that "the real measure of how civilized we are is the way we choose to punish people. It's not civilized to tell somebody 'you're going to sit in the stocks and we're going to throw stones at you.'" Carl F. Horowitz, Washington correspondent for *Investor's Business Daily*, has also attacked shaming, a category in which he includes public hangings, beheadings of drug dealers, blacklists, and boycotts.

Justifying Shame

When I faced similar challenges from the students in a sociology class I teach at George Washington University, I suggested that an examination of shaming suffers if one places the label on all punitive measures of which one disapproves. True or pure shaming involves only symbolic acts that communicate censure, ranging from relatively gentle expressions such as according a student a C+ or sending a disruptive kid to stand in the classroom's corner, to more severe measures such as facing the victims of one's assault in close quarters and then apologizing to them in front of the community. Shaming differs sharply from many other modes of punishment—public flogging, for instance—in that the latter inflict bodily harm rather than being limited to psychic discomfort. While shaming has some untoward consequences of its own, it is a relatively light punishment, especially if one takes into account that most other penalties shame in addition to inflicting their designated hurt.

I stressed to my class that shaming is morally appropriate or justified only when those being shamed are acting out of free will. When people act in ways that the law or prevailing mores consider inappropriate, but cannot help themselves from doing so (for example, when those with mental illnesses defecate in the streets or scream loudly at 3:00 A.M.), chiding them is highly inappropriate. They are to be helped, removed if need be, but hardly shamed. . . .

At the end of the day, some form of disincentive—sparing, let us hope, and mostly of the gentle kind—cannot be avoided. Or, as Texas State District Judge Ted Poe, a strong proponent of shaming penalties, puts it, "a little shame goes a long way. Some folks say everyone should have high self-esteem, but that's not the real world. Sometimes people should feel bad."

The Penalty of Crime

Having to pay a fine isn't likely to make a difference in a person's behavior, especially if the person has enough money to pay without any significant harm to his or her bank account. Subjecting them to the indignity of having their crime become public knowledge by making them perform public restitution is more likely to have a deterrent effect. With any luck, these people will feel that the penalties for the crime they have committed outweigh any possible benefits and not make the same mistake twice.

Rick Reinstein, *West Michigan University Herald*, April 8, 1998.

An often overlooked feature of shaming, I should add, is that it is deeply democratic. Shaming reflects the community's values and hence cannot be imposed by the authorities against a people. Thus, if being sent to the principal's office is a badge of honor in a boy's peer culture, no shaming will occur in that situation. A yellow star, imposed to mark and shame Jews in Nazi Germany, is now worn as a matter of pride in Israel. Thus, people are protected better from shaming that reflects values that are not shared by their community than from other forms of punishment, punishment that can be imposed by authorities without the specific consent of those who are governed. . . .

The History of Shaming
The history of our country offers some lessons on how shaming works, especially on what happens to a good thing

when it is driven too far—much too far. Most important, our past teaches us the significance of the particular context. In colonial America, shaming was very common, not merely one tool of punishment among others but a major one. Indeed, historians report that it worked so well in some colonies—South Carolina, for instance—that no prisons were deemed necessary. (This applied only to white people; slaves were treated far more savagely.)

The purest form of shaming was "admonition." The legal scholar Adam Hirsch describes it as follows:

> Faced with a community member who had committed a serious offense, the magistrates or clergymen would lecture him privately to elicit his repentance and a resolution to reform. The offender would then be brought into open court for formal admonition by the magistrate, a public confession of wrongdoing, and a pronouncement of sentence, wholly or partially suspended to symbolize the community's forgiveness.

"The aim," writes historian Lawrence M. Friedman, "was not just to punish, but to teach a lesson, so that the sinful sheep would want to get back to the flock." Friedman also describes another common shaming measure: requiring the culprit—a thief, for example—to wear for six months

> a "Roman T, not less than four inches long and one inch wide, of a scarlet colour, on the outside of the outermost garment, upon the back, between the shoulders, so that all times to be fully exposed to view, for a badge of his or her crime." A robber had to wear a scarlet R; and a forger, a scarlet F, "at least six inches long and two inches wide."

While I can't vouch for Nathaniel Hawthorne's scarlet A, there are cases on record of an adulteress sentenced to wear the letter B (presumably for "bawd") and an adulterous couple forced to wear the letters AD.

Throughout New England, and on occasion as far south as Virginia, stocks (frameworks that secured the ankles and sometimes the wrists) and pillories (posts that secured the head and hands) were set up in town squares in order to maximize the public nature of the offenders' humiliation. Stocks and pillories were effective shaming devices, but they also imposed an excessively cruel degree of physical discomfort by exposing the criminal to the elements and restricting his movements. And, like shaming insignia, they were often accompanied by corporal punishment. In fact, some pillories were used specifically to restrain offenders while they were lashed.

One reason shaming was so powerful in colonial America is that it took place in communities that were much smaller, more tightly knit, and more moralistic than any here today. Friedman describes them as "little worlds on their own, cut off from each other" in which "small-town life [was] at its most communal—inbred and extremely gossipy." Historian Roger Thompson writes that Massachusetts communities were "well stocked with moral monitors who did not miss much in the goldfish-bowl existence of daily life." For example, single people who moved into some colonies were required to board with someone so that the community could keep an eye on them. In such an environment, six months under the stigma of a scarlet letter or even a single day in the stocks—exposed to the scorn of almost everyone one knew—could easily have been very distressing.

In contrast, many Americans today are members of two or more communities (for instance, at work and in their home neighborhoods) and psychologically can shift much of their ego involvement from a community that unduly chastens them to another. While it was not practical during colonial times for most people to escape from one community to another, today the average American moves about once every five years, and in the process chooses to which community he or she is willing to be subjected. Moreover, privacy at home is much greater, and the moral agenda of most communities is almost incomparably briefer. . . .

Give Shaming a Fair Try

Of all the colonial methods of shaming, only admonition placed a strong emphasis on reintegrative justice. Its example should appeal to the progressive criminologists who seek to restore it, although for others it may evoke the image of a Soviet or Chinese trial. (Having witnessed a trial in Shanghai, I was offended most not by the shaming per se but by the kinds of "crimes" people were shamed for, which included conceiving a second child and listening to the BBC [British Broadcasting Corporation].) But because shaming was so often linked with public flogging—the sort of cruel and unusual punishment most of us abhorred when a young American was caned in Singapore in 1994—it is easy to see why its history has left it in ill repute. I believe it would be more productive to think about the ways our more liberal and tolerant society might adapt shaming to our needs than to be swayed by its anachronistic image.

Most important, no social policy should be evaluated in itself; it should be compared with the alternatives. Our criminal justice system jails millions of people, about half of them for non-violent crimes. Offenders are incarcerated for ever longer periods, in harsher conditions, with fewer opportunities for parole. Despite its increasing rigor, the system rehabilitates very few and the recidivism rate is very high. And when a year in jail costs about the same as a year at one of our nation's most expensive colleges, taxpayers bear a heavy burden. Our society is therefore eager to find more effective, more humane, and cheaper modes of deterrence. I have no desire to bring back pillories or other restraining devices, but does it make sense to reject shaming—a strictly symbolic punishment—without giving it a fair try?

"The crude treatment of shame [in sentencing] . . . could be a catastrophe."

Shame-Based Punishment May Not Be an Effective Alternative

Suzanne M. Retzinger and Thomas J. Scheff

Searching for innovative, cost-effective sentencing, some courts have experimented with using shame to punish offenders and reduce crime. In the following viewpoint, Suzanne M. Retzinger and Thomas J. Scheff argue that shame-based punishment may not be an effective alternative to prison. The authors assert that shame is a complex emotion and current shame-based punishments ignore the harmful psychological consequences that an individual may experience after shaming. Therefore, the "crude" use of shame may backfire and do little to deter crime. If shaming is used, the authors recommend that it must be applied in a way that does not humiliate offenders and allows for their re-integration in the community. Retzinger is a family relations mediator at the Superior Court in Ventura, California. Scheff is a sociologist and professor at the University of California, Santa Barbara.

As you read, consider the following questions:
1. According to the authors, what are the four steps taken in a conference?
2. How do Retzinger and Scheff support their claim that "branding" offenders may be counterproductive?
3. In Retzinger and Scheff's opinion, what action is necessary to "manage shame beneficially"?

Excerpted from "Shame and Shaming in Restorative Justice," by Suzanne M. Retzinger and Thomas J. Scheff, www.tryoung.journal-pomocrim/vol-8/scheff.html. Reprinted with permission from Thomas J. Scheff.

In the last several years, the idea of shaming offenders as an alternative to imprisonment has been widely discussed, and in some jurisdictions, even implemented. Although it is gratifying to see shame being taken seriously, we have serious reservations about most of the discussions and implementations of this idea.

At the heart of the current discussion of shaming offenders is the assumption that shame is a simple emotion that comes in only two sizes: shame or no shame. But actually shame is a complex emotion which comes in many shapes, sizes, and degrees of intensity. Legal scholars and judges who treat shame as merely binary are in a position of a skier who makes no distinction between the many kinds of snow. Just as lack of knowledge of types of snow may lead a skier to disaster, so the crude treatment of shame in current discussions could be a catastrophe.

In this viewpoint we propose that the only kind of shame which is uniformly effective in restorative justice is shame that comes from within the offender. Conversely, shame that is imposed without almost always hardens the offenders against reconciliation and restoration of the damage done. . . .

Why Conferences?

It is widely recognized that the court/prison route is both expensive and not very effective in controlling crime. Evidence is now available that victim-offender mediation is not only cheaper than court and prison, but also more effective in decreasing recidivism. One of the great advantages of mediation is that in the confrontation between offender and victim, the offender confesses his crime, is likely to recognize its consequences for the victim, and therefore to accept responsibility for his actions. For the most part, the court/prison system encourages offenders to deny their responsibility, which may be one of the reasons for high rates of recidivism.

However, mediation of offender-victims conflict, even at its most effective, is still only a way of dealing with crimes that have already occurred. Mediation does not directly prevent crime, even though it probably has indirect preventive effects. As an initiative in crime prevention, courses on mediation for young people early in their schooling will be discussed later in this viewpoint. Mediation of offenses in schools prior to police intervention, and developing courses on mediation would be a way of involving educational institutions into a program for dealing with crime and violence. The introduction of mediation courses and community conferences in educational institutions would be another way of bringing more of the community to participate in the control of crime and violence.

Conferencing also may be relevant to the problem of youth gangs, since its extended format allows for bringing together gang members with the families and officials of a neighborhood or community. Such a meeting might lead to discussion, and even resolution, of more fundamental problems than just the particular offense that led to the conference. At the very least some of the conflict in values between the gang and the community could be aired. Such a meeting might be as educational for the community as for the gang.

The conference procedure promises both to reduce the cost of crime control and to make it more effective. To the extent that police forces become involved, conferences could transform their attitudes toward their job and toward offenders, since it allows them to see offenders and victims as human beings. . . .

The conference format typically involves four steps. First, the offender describes his or her offense in detail. Next, the facilitator asks the offender to describe the consequences of the offense, how it affected him, and how it affected the victim and others. Thirdly, the victim and the victim's supporters tell how the crime affected them. This step is often highly emotional, with visible tears and/or anger. The last part of the conference is working out a settlement, one that will be acceptable to both victim and offender. . . .

But conferences are not useful for truth-finding. For crimes in which significant facts are in dispute, there is still no substitute for a court trial. Courts of law are truth machines: the adversarial system and the rules of evidence are necessary for cases in which facts are disputed. The court system is the best mechanism we have for dealing with such conflict. However, if the facts are not disputed—that is, if there is a confession or a plea bargain—then the cumbersome and expensive court machinery is unnecessary. A large majority of criminal cases are disposed without trial (either by confession or by plea bargain). The large array of highly paid professional personnel—judges, attorneys, court reporters, bailiffs, etc.—need not be involved in the majority of cases.

This is not to say courts and prisons are not necessary. Their very existence leads to many confessions and plea bargains because many if not most offenders confess or plea bargain in order to avoid trial and imprisonment. The existing court system serves many necessary functions. But it no longer need be the first line of defense against crime. . . .

Reintegrative Steps Are Necessary

A framework for community conferences can found in [Australian criminologist John] Braithwaite's concept of reintegrative shaming: enough shaming to bring home the seriousness of the offense, but not so much as to humiliate and harden. There was a time in England when thieves were punished by branding their foreheads with the letter "F" (for felon). This punishment actually led to an increase in crime: since the branded felons were excluded from ordinary life, they had no alternative but to become professional thieves and highwaymen. The symbolic branding of the offender is one of the key pitfalls not only of the court/prison system, but also of the community conference: too much shame can be just as destructive as too little. . . .

For conferences to be maximally effective, two separate movements of shame should occur. First, all shame must be removed from the victim. The humiliation of degradation, betrayal and violation that has been inflicted on the victim can be relieved. This step is a key element in the victim's future well-being; it is the shame component, the feeling that the victim has that if only she had acted differently, the crime wouldn't have occurred or would have been less painful, that leads to the most intense and protracted suffering. The usual handling of crimes through courts and imprisonment does very little to relieve the victim of her suffering. Perhaps this is the main reason that many victims and much of the voting public want to visit excessive punishment on offenders, to make them suffer as their victims suffer.

The removal of shame from the victim is accomplished by making sure that all of the shame connected with the crime is accepted by the offender. By acknowledging his complete responsibility for the crime, the offender not only takes the first step toward rehabilitation, but also eases the suffering of the victim. For the shaming of the offender to be reintegrative, however, the facilitator must take care that it not be excessive, as already indicated. Humiliating the offender in the conference makes it almost impossible for him both to accept responsibility and to help remove shame from the victim. . . .

An Extreme Option

Shame is just one of many alternative-sentencing options, and it is extreme, according to Herbert Hoelter, director of the Center on Institutions. "Shame cases are more for judges who are looking for a political answer to a sentence rather than a thoughtful one," Hoelter said. "They are not part of the everyday fabric. They are anomalies within the criminal justice system." Critics say shame-based sentencing causes psychological damage and that the crime should be stigmatized, not the criminal.

Julie Deardorff, *Chicago Tribune*, April 12, 2000.

In order to manage shame beneficially, it is necessary to recover the positive, reconciliative uses of normal shame from the maws of repression and silence, and to relearn its value as a powerful emotion for forming community. "The very fact that shame is an isolating experience also means that if one can find ways of sharing and communicating it, this communication can bring about particular closeness with others. . . ." [Helen Lynd]. The idea expressed in this passage is crucially significant for community conferences: if the offender can come to the point of "sharing and communicating" his shame instead of hiding or denying it, the damage to the bond between the offender and the other participants may be repaired.

The nature of the formal apology in community conferences provides a good example of the crucial part that acknowledging shame plays in the drama of conflict and reconciliation. Formal apologies are an important step in all forms of victim-offender mediation. The chances that conferences produce healing and repair are significantly linked to the quality of the apology, its genuineness. . . .

Mediation, Not Only Shaming

We have urged that community conferences be tried as an alternative to courts and prisons in those cases where offenders have confessed. This approach promises to be a more effective, and certainly a less expensive way of managing these types of cases, easily a majority of offenders. This approach may also have many desirable side-effects, such as helping to rebuild community and transform police attitudes.

However, community conferencing is only an indirect approach to crime prevention. To attack the problem close to its roots, it may be also desirable to introduce mediation and conferencing into elementary and secondary schools and colleges. The first step would be to develop classes based on mediation ideas and skills. The direct effect of such classes would be to give students skills in negotiation and peace-making. These skills would serve students their entire lives, enabling them to communicate and negotiate their needs, and settle their differences peacefully, avoiding subterfuge and violent confrontation. . . .

When taught properly, mediation courses are highly dramatic and would probably be popular. Through the use of role-playing, students would exchange roles, playing the parts of the victim, offender and facilitator alternately. In this way, they would learn to view disputes from different viewpoints, not only their own. This experience, of understanding the world from others' points of view, is an important building block of community.

Periodical Bibliography

The following articles have been selected to supplement the diverse views presented in this chapter. Addresses are provided for periodicals not indexed in the *Readers' Guide to Periodical Literature*, the *Alternative Press Index*, the *Social Sciences Index*, or the *Index to Legal Periodicals and Books*.

Hector Becerra and Hudson Sangree	"Sentenced to Serve," *Los Angeles Times*, December 3, 1999. Available from Reprints, Times Mirror Square, Los Angeles, CA 90053 or www.latimes.com.
John J. DiIulio Jr. and Joseph P. Tierney	"An Easy Ride for Felons on Probation," *The New York Times*, August 29, 2000.
Jean S. Harris	"Jail Sentences with No End," *The New York Times*, May 20, 1999.
John Irwin, Vincent Schiraldi, and Jason Zeidenburg	"America's One Million Nonviolent Prisoners," *Social Justice*, Summer 2000.
Arthur J. Lurigio, David E. Olson, and James A. Swartz	"Chicago Day-Reporting Center Reduces Pretrial Detention, Drug Use, and Absconding," *Overcrowded Times*, February 1998. Available from PO Box 110, Castine, MN 55082-0055.
George Miller	"A Smart Solution to Jail Overcrowding," *Corrections Today*, July 2000. Available from the American Correctional Association, 4380 Forbes Blvd., Lanham, MD 20706-4322.
Jean Russell	"Shame! Shame! Shame!," *Good Housekeeping*, August 1997.
Peter Slevin	"Arizona's Anti-Drug Gamble: Taking Jail Out of the Equation; Treatment Focus Yields Benefits, but Critics Say Prison Is a Key Option," *Washington Post*, October 20, 2000. Available from 1150 Fifteenth St. NW, Washington, DC 20071.
Tom Stuckey	"Home Detention Under Fire; PG Slaying Stokes Debate on How to Regulate Monitoring," *Washington Times*, June 28, 1999. Available at 3600 New York Ave. NE, Washington, DC 20002 or www.washtimes.com.

For Further Discussion

Chapter 1

1. How does Patrick F. Fagan and Robert E. Moffit's view of the effect of social programs on crime differ from Elliot Currie's view? In your opinion, whose argument is stronger, and why?

2. Todd R. Clear claims that the view of crime as a phenomenon of individuals is "simplistic." In your opinion, does Morgan Reynolds hold this view of crime? Provide examples from the viewpoints.

3. Jeff Becker argues that profiting from prisons does not present a "conflict of interest" because a private prison must be managed well to be profitable. Barry Yeoman contends private companies prioritize profits over the well-being of inmates. In your opinion, is it unethical to profit from the prison system? Why or why not?

Chapter 2

1. Francis T. Murphy claims that a punitive penal policy asserts the consequences of adhering to or defying moral values and that rehabilitation efforts in prisons have weakened the effectiveness of the criminal justice system. Do you agree with Murphy? Why or why not?

2. Mara Taub describes the extreme surroundings and harsh treatment experienced by some prisoners in a supermax prison. Do you believe that offenders should be placed in supermaxes? Does the fact that the safety of the general inmate population and prison staff must be protected change your opinion? Why or why not?

3. Roger Stubblefield argues that the purpose of imprisonment is to punish offenders and that the prison system has strayed too far from this ideal. Jess Maghan claims that prisons have become the extension of social programs, and he approves of the services and amenities available to inmates. In your opinion, which author makes the more persuasive argument? Provide examples from the viewpoints.

Chapter 3

1. Warren Richey asserts that inmate activist groups like PRIDE, a nonprofit prison industry organization, back prison labor. However, Gordon Lafer argues that big businesses seeking the "ultimate flexible and disciplined workforce" support prison labor. In your opinion, who has the most to gain from prison in-

dustries, working inmates, or the private companies that hire them? Provide examples from the viewpoints.

2. Tracey Meares claims that there is an "unambiguous historical connection" between today's chain gangs and black slavery. Jayce Warman suggests that a "modified" chain gang can perform community service and build inmates' self-esteem. In your opinion, can chain gangs be humane? Why or why not?

Chapter 4

1. Joseph M. Bessette argues that violent offenders do not deserve parole. In your opinion, should inmates convicted of violent crimes be paroled for outstanding behavior and progress in prison? Why or why not?

2. Charles L. Hobson contends that the lessening of penalties for drug possession by Proposition 36 is the "virtual decriminalization" of drug use. In your opinion, does this initiative decriminalize drug abuse? Provide examples from the viewpoints.

3. David Mulholland claims that creative sentencing can serve the community by protecting the public without imprisoning the offender. For instance, a man convicted of child molestation was sentenced to place a sign in front of his house warning children to stay away. Do you agree with the author that these creative sentences should be enforced? Does the fact that some creative sentences may infringe upon an offender's Constitutional rights influence your opinion? Why or why not?

4. Amitai Etzioni contends that the power of shame can effectively deter crime. In your opinion, should shaming be used even though it can be psychologically damaging to an offender? Why or why not?

Organizations to Contact

The editors have compiled the following list of organizations concerned with the issues debated in this book. The descriptions are
derived from materials provided by the organizations. All have
publications or information available for interested readers. The
list was compiled on the date of publication of the present volume;
the information provided here may change. Be aware that many
organizations take several weeks or longer to respond to inquiries,
so allow as much time as possible.

American Civil Liberties Union (ACLU)
National Prison Project
125 Broad St., New York, NY 10004-2400
(212) 549-2500 • fax: (212) 549-2646
e-mail: aclu@aclu.org • website: www.aclu.org

Formed in 1972, the project serves as a national resource center
and litigates cases to strengthen and protect adult and juvenile offenders' Eighth Amendment rights. It opposes electronic monitoring of offenders and the privatization of prisons. The project
publishes the quarterly *National Prison Project Journal* and various
booklets.

American Correctional Association (ACA)
4380 Forbes Blvd., Lanham, MD 20706-4322
(800) 222-5646 • fax: (301) 918-1900
e-mail: jeffw@aca.org • website: www.corrections.com/aca

The ACA is committed to improving national and international
correctional policy and to promoting the professional development
of those working in the field of corrections. It offers a variety of
books and correspondence courses on corrections and criminal justice and publishes the bimonthly magazine *Corrections Today*.

Bureau of Prisons
320 First St. NW, Washington, DC 20534
(202) 307-3198 (at the Office of Public Affairs)
e-mail: webmaster@bop.gov • website: www.bop.gov

The bureau works to protect society by confining offenders in the
controlled environments of prison and community-based facilities.
It believes in providing work and other self-improvement opportunities within these facilities to assist offenders in becoming law-
abiding citizens. The bureau publishes the book *The State of the
Bureau*.

Campaign for an Effective Crime Policy
514 Tenth St. NW, Washington, DC 20004
(202) 628-1903 • fax: (202) 628-1091
e-mail: staff@crimepolicy.org • website: www.crimepolicy.org
Coordinated by the Sentencing Project, the campaign's purpose is to promote information, ideas, discussion, and debate about criminal justice policy and to move sentencing policy toward alternative sentencing. The campaign's core document is *A Call for a Rational Debate on Crime and Punishment.*

Center for Alternative Sentencing and Employment Services (CASES)
346 Broadway, New York, NY 10013
(212) 732-0076 • fax: (212) 571-0292
e-mail: casesinfo@cases.org • website: www.cases.org
CASES seeks to end what it views as the overuse of incarceration as a response to crime. It operates two alternative-sentence programs in New York City: the Court Employment Project, which provides intensive supervision and services for felony offenders, and the Community Service Sentencing Project, which works with repeat misdemeanor offenders. The center advocates in court for such offenders' admission into its programs. CASES publishes various program brochures.

Fortune Society
53 W 23rd St., New York, NY 10010
(212) 691-7554 • fax: (212) 255-4948
e-mail: info@fortunesociety.org • website: www.fortunesociety.org
The society is an organization of ex-offenders and others interested in penal reform. It is dedicated to educating the public about prisons, criminal justice issues, and the root causes of crime. The society also works to help former prisoners break the cycle of crime and incarceration. Its publications include the quarterly *Fortune News.*

The Heritage Foundation
214 Massachusetts Ave. NE, Washington, DC 20002
(202) 546-4400 • fax: (202) 546-8328
e-mail: info@heritage.org • website: www.heritage.org
The Heritage Foundation is a conservative public policy research institute. It is a proponent of limited government and advocates tougher sentencing and the construction of more prisons. The foundation publishes articles on a variety of public policy issues in its *Backgrounder* series and in its quarterly journal *Policy Review.*

Justice Fellowship
PO Box 16069, Washington, DC 20041-6069
(703) 904-7312 • fax: (703) 478-9679
e-mail: mail@justicefellowship.org
website: www.justicefellowship.org

The Justice Fellowship is a national criminal justice reform organization that advocates victims' rights, alternatives to prison, and community involvement in the criminal justice system. It aims to make the criminal justice system more consistent with biblical teachings on justice. It publishes the brochures *A Case for Alternatives to Prison*, *A Case for Prison Industries*, *A Case for Victims' Rights*, and *Beyond Crime and Punishment: Restorative Justice*, as well as the quarterly newsletter *Justice Report*.

Law Enforcement Alliance of America (LEAA)
7700 Leesburg Pike, Suite 421, Falls Church, VA 22043
(800) 766-8578 • fax: (703) 556-6485
website: www.leaa.org/index.htm

LEAA is a nonprofit, nonpartisan advocacy organization made up of law enforcement professionals, crime victims, and concerned citizens dedicated to making America safer from crime. It provides assistance to law enforcement professionals, promotes victims' rights over criminals' rights, supports criminal justice reform that targets violent criminals, and opposes gun control. It publishes the quarterly magazine *LEAA Advocate*, which periodically addresses correctional issues.

National Association of Chiefs of Police (NACP)
3801 Biscayne Blvd., Miami, FL 33137
(305) 573-0070 • fax: (305) 573-9819
website: www.aphf.org

NACP is a nonprofit educational organization of police chiefs and command law enforcement officers. It provides consultation and research services in all phases of police activity. NACP publishes the bimonthly magazine the *Chief of Police* as well as an annual spring survey of command law enforcement officers.

National Center for Policy Analysis (NCPA)

Dallas Headquarters: 12655 N. Central Expy., Suite 720, Dallas, TX 75243-1739
(972) 386-6272 • fax: (972) 386-0924
Washington Office: 655 15th St. NW, Suite 375, Washington, DC 20005
(202) 628-6671 • fax: (202) 628-6474
e-mail: ncpa@ncpa.org • website: www.npca.org

Based in Dallas, Texas, this nonprofit, nonpartisan research institute has been publishing studies on a wide array of public policies since 1983. NCPA works to reform public policies, from Social Security to the prison system. Its prison-related publications include the studies "Privatizing Probation and Parole," "Factories Behind Bars," and its annual report, "Crime and Punishment in America."

National Center on Institutions and Alternatives (NCIA)

3125 Mount Vernon Ave., Alexandria, VA 22305
(703) 684-0373 • fax: (703) 684-6037
e-mail: info@ncianet.org • website: www.igc.org/ncia

NCIA is a criminal justice foundation that encourages community-based alternatives to prison that are more effective in providing education, training, and personal skills required for the rehabilitation of nonviolent offenders. The center advocates doubling "good conduct" credit for the early release of nonviolent first-time offenders in the federal system to make room for violent offenders. NCIA publications include the reports "As Millennium Approaches, 1 Million African Americans Behind Bars" and "Twenty Years Later: Scared Straight Still Doesn't Have It."

Prisoners' Rights Union (PRU)

PO Box 1019, Sacramento, CA 95812-1019

The PRU's primary goal is to educate California prisoners about their civil rights and to ensure human rights for all prisoners. It publishes the *California State Prisoner's Handbook* and the quarterly newspaper *California Prisoner*, which reports on the current status of legislative and judicial decisions that affect the lives of prisoners and their families.

RAND Corporation

1700 Main St., PO Box 2138, Santa Monica, CA 90407-2138
(310) 393-0411 • fax: (310) 393-4818
e-mail: correspondence@rand.org • website: www.rand.org

The RAND Corporation is an independent, nonprofit organization engaged in research on national security issues and the public welfare. It conducts its work with support from federal, state, and local governments and from foundations and other philanthropic sources. It published the reports "Three Strikes and You're Out: Estimated Benefits and Costs of California's New Mandatory-Sentencing Law" and "Drug Offenders and the Criminal Justice System: Will Proposition 36 Treat or Create Problems?"

The Sentencing Project

514 Tenth St. NW, Suite 1000, Washington, DC 20004
(202) 628-0871 • fax: (202) 628-1091
e-mail: staff@sentencingproject.org
website: www.sentencingproject.org

The project seeks to provide public defenders and other public officials with information on establishing and improving alternative sentencing programs that provide convicted persons with positive and constructive options to incarceration. It promotes increased public understanding of the sentencing process and alternative sentencing programs. The Sentencing Project recently published the reports "Losing the Vote: The Impact of Felony Disenfranchisement Law in the United States" and "Diminishing Returns: Crime and Incarceration in the 1990s."

Bibliography of Books

Howard Abadinsky · *Probation and Parole.* Upper Saddle River, NJ: Prentice-Hall, 1999.

Mumia Abu-Jamal · *All Things Censored.* New York: Seven Stories Press, 2000.

David C. Anderson · *Sensible Justice: Alternatives to Prison.* New York: New Press, 1998.

James F. Anderson, Laronistine Dyson, and Jerald C. Burns · *Boot Camps: An Intermediate Sanction.* Lanham, MD: University Press of America, 2000.

D.A. Andrews and James Bonta · *The Psychology of Criminal Conduct.* Cincinnati, OH: Anderson, 1998.

Joe Arpaio and Len Sherman · *America's Toughest Sheriff: How We Can Win the War Against Crime.* Arlington, TX: Summit, 1996.

Daniel Burton-Rose, Dan Pens, and Paul Wright, eds. · *The Celling of America: An Inside Look at the U.S. Prison Industry.* Monroe, ME: Common Courage Press, 1998.

Scott Christianson · *With Liberty for Some: 500 Years of Imprisonment in America.* Boston: Northeastern University Press, 1998.

David Cole · *No Equal Justice: Race and Class in the American Criminal Justice System.* New York: New Press, 2000.

Ted Conover · *Newjack: Guarding Sing Sing.* New York: Random House, 2000.

H. Bruce Franklin · *Prison Writing in Twentieth-Century America.* New York: Penguin, 1998.

Steve Gravett · *Drugs in Prison.* New York: Continuum, 2001.

Richard Harding · *Private Prisons and Public Accountability.* Piscataway, NJ: Transaction, 1997.

Michael Jacobson Hardy · *Behind the Razor Wire: Portrait of a Contemporary American Prison System.* New York: New York University Press, 1998.

Robert Johnson · *Hard Time: Understanding and Reforming the Prison.* Belmont, CA: Wadsworth, 1995.

Don A. Josi and Dale K. Sechrest · *The Changing Career of the Correctional Officer.* Woburn, MA: Butterworth-Heinemann, 1998.

Nathan Kantrowitz · *Close Control: Managing a Maximum Security Prison: The Story of Ragen's Stateville Penitentiary.* Albany, NY: Harrow and Heston, 1996.

Kenneth Kerle	*American Jails: Looking to the Future*. Woburn, MA: Butterworth-Heinemann, 1998.
Mark Mauer	*Race to Incarcerate*. New York: New Press, 1999.
John P. May and Khalid R. Pitts, eds.	*Building Violence: How America's Rush to Incarcerate Creates More Violence*. Thousand Oaks, CA: Sage, 1999.
James McGrath Morris	*Jailhouse Journalism: The Fourth Estate Behind Bars*. Jefferson, NC: McFarland, 1998.
Norval Morris and David Rothman, eds.	*The Oxford History of Prisons: The Practice of Punishment in Western Society*. New York: Oxford University Press, 1995.
Christian Parenti	*Lockdown America: Police and Prisons in the Age of Crisis*. Cambridge, MA: South End Press, 1998.
Vernon L. Quinsey, Grant Thomas Harris, Marnie E. Rice, and Catherine A. Cormier	*Violent Offenders: Appraising and Management Risk (Law and Public Policy)*. Washington, DC: American Psychological Association, 1998.
Edward E. Rhine, ed.	*Best Practices: Excellence in Corrections*. Lanham, MD: American Correctional Association, 1998.
Elihu Rosenblatt	*Criminal Injustice: Confronting the Prison Crisis*. Cambridge, MA: South End Press, 1998.
Stanton E. Samenow	*Straight Talk About Criminals*. North Bergen, NJ: Jason Aronson, 1998.
Clive Sharp	*How to Survive Federal Prison Camp: A Guidebook for Those Caught Up in the System*. Port Townsend, WA: Loompanics Unlimited, 1997.
Michael Tonry	*Sentencing Reform in Overcrowded Times*. New York: Oxford University Press, 1997.
Claudia Whitman, ed., Julie Zimmerman, and Tekla Miller	*Frontiers of Justice: Coddling or Common Sense? (Frontiers of Justice Vol. 2)*. Brunswick, ME: Biddle, 1998.

Index

Abramson, Jeffrey, 168
African Americans
  and chain gangs, 131–32
  criminal record remaining with, 25–26
  incarceration rate for, 19, 25, 26, 34, 42–43
  in supermax prisons, 98
  unemployed, 47–48
Anacostia Men's Employment Network (AMEN), 143
Aranella, Peter, 174

Becker, Jeff, 66
Bennett, William J., 16
Berlin, Isaiah, 84
Beshara, Anthony, 75
Bessette, Joseph M., 145
Bidinotto, Robert, 56
Blumstein, Alfred, 27
Braithwaite, John, 184
Bronstein, Alvin, 54
Broward Correctional Institution, 113, 114
Broward Optical, 115, 116
Brown, Joe B., 164, 165–66

California Bail Agents, 154
California Correctional Peace Officers Association (CCPOA), 154
California Probation, Parole, and Correctional Association, 154
Carver, Jay, 142
Cash, David, 174
chain gangs
  as appropriate vs. cruel punishment, 128–29
  beginning of, 125
  as cost effective, 127
    con, 132–33
  as deterring crime, 127–28
    con, 132
  vs. education and training, 134
  historical connection between slavery and, 131–32
  inmate freedom gained from, 126
  inmates on, 133
  vs. preserving humanity of

people, 134–35
  rehabilitation through, 125–27
  as risk to the public, 133–34
  states using, 125, 131
Cherminsky, Erwin, 176
children
  illegitimate, 31–32
  influence of imprisonment on, 63
Chin, Vincent, 148
Clark, Ramsey, 150
Clear, Todd R., 57
Clinton, Bill, 15
Cole, David, 16
community conferences, 182–84, 185–86
Corral, Jaime, 166–67
Correction Corporation of America (CCA), 67, 72–76
Court Services and Offender Supervision Agency, 141
creative sentencing. See sentencing, alternative
crime
  American public's simplistic view on, 88
  causes of
    family breakdown, 32–34
    probation and parole abuse, 37–38
  as a concept dilemma, 88–90
  gangs
    and community conferencing, 183
    incarceration does not influence, 60
    rehabilitation does not work for, 55
  race is not a factor in, 34–35
  rate of, 33
    correlated with incarceration rate, 21–22, 36–37, 50–51, 52–53, 56
    is not influenced by incarceration, 44, 58, 89
    geographic differences, 14, 44–46
    indirect ways imprisonment increases, 63–65

groups opposing, 121–23
human potential realized
  through, 114
inmates' lack of rights for,
  119–20
lack of benefits for, 119
and overseas labor, 114–15,
  120–21
supporters of, 121
as threat to private-sector
  workers, 120
types of jobs for, 120
wages for, 114, 119
work ethic developed from, 116
see also chain gangs
mentally ill, 48
modern facilities for, 106
in private prisons, as violent and
  dangerous, 73–75
services for
  changing, danger in, 107–108
  elimination of, 106
  importance of, 108–109
in supermax prisons, 92
  brutal treatment of, 96–98, 99
  conditions of, 92
  types of, 97–98
  violation of rights of, 92–93, 94
suppressing criminal element in,
  103–104
treatment of, history of, 101
warped socialization of, 29–30
weight training by, 80
see also criminals; offenders
Ivanko, Katarina, 87
Iverson, Sherrice, 174

Jackson, Jesse, 60
Jackson, Peter L., 140–41
judges
  and creative sentencing, 171–72
  leniency by, 148

Kappelhoff, Mark, 175–76
Kee, Sylvia, 115
Kelley, W.R., 60
Klein, Malcolm, 55

labor. *See* inmates, as labor
Lafer, Gordon, 118
Lampson, Nicholas, 174
Langan, Patrick A., 19

law enforcement, 33
Lea, Jeff, 143
legislation
  on inmate labor, 120
  on pretrial release, 38
  on prisoner lawsuits, 93, 94
Levitt, Steve, 14
Lewis, Jean, 150
Liberty Correctional Institution,
  115
Loconte, Joe, 166
Loo, H.J., 60
Lotke, Eric, 143
Lott, John, 50
Louisiana Pacific, 123
Lynd, Staughton, 75

Maghan, Jess, 105
Marcone, Paul, 76
marriage, absence of, 34
Mauer, Mark, 164
McCollum, Bill, 23
McNulty, Paul, 164
Meares, Tracey L., 130
mediation, 182–84
Medlin, Jason, 76
Menninger, Karl, 150
mental health care, 48
Mikulski, Barbara, 32
Miller, Jerome, 24
minorities. *See* African Americans;
  Hispanics
Moffit, Robert E., 31
monitoring, 138
Moore, Margaret, 74
Moran, Richard, 23
Morris, Eugene, 128–29
Mulholland, David, 163
Munroe High School (Northridge,
  CA), 166
Murphy, Francis T., 81
Murray, Charles, 52–53, 54

Nagin, Daniel, 50
Nitz, Michael, 148

offenders
  drug
    African American, 25, 42–43
    prison time is necessary for, 161
    and repeat offenses, 36
    and replacement of criminals, 60

199